Beginners Investor Guide To Crypto and Trading

Trading Cryptocurrency for Beginners

Oscar Hawthorn

Table of Contents

Glossary

References

Introduction

The mention of cryptocurrency always elicits controversial views. People have divergent views on all aspects of this market, from its financial value to its utility and sustainability. Notably, when most people talk about cryptocurrency, their discussions tend to center around Bitcoin. Granted, Bitcoin is by far the most famous and popular cryptocurrency. Since it was launched in 2009, Bitcoin has taken the world by storm, grown, and achieved incredible milestones. However, in the grand scheme of cryptocurrency and blockchain technology, Bitcoin is but a drop in the ocean.

There's more to cryptocurrency than just Bitcoin. Discussing cryptocurrency from a Bitcoin point of view is quite limiting because we restrict ourselves to a fraction of the financial aspect of it. There are hundreds, if not thousands, of cryptocurrencies currently available on the market. What we need to understand is that there's enormous potential, not just in cryptocurrency, but in the entire blockchain ecosystem that we are yet to explore. With this approach, you have a better chance of making a successful foray into trading cryptocurrencies because you go in with an open mind.

Going in with an open mind means awareness of not just the opportunities available, but also the pitfalls. Some people still believe that cryptocurrency is nothing but a fad, a bubble that will burst, leaving the masses staring at a bottomless pit of losses. Given the controversial events that have taken place in the cryptocurrency market over the years, you wouldn't blame them. Everyone has a right to their opinion on cryptocurrency, particularly since many governments have mostly been apprehensive about the whole idea.

On the other hand, we cannot also turn a blind eye to the fact that people are making fortunes by trading in cryptocurrencies, and this is just from the monetary aspect. Casting our gaze beyond finance, we introduce concepts like NFTs, the metaverse, decentralized finance products, and many other blockchain solutions that have proven quite effective where they've been implemented. What we have in our presence is revolutionary technology whose impact and influence transcend the traditional financial market. The applications of blockchain technology have spread far and wide into other sectors of our economy and society, like politics, the industrial sector, retail, media, healthcare, and even environmental science.

Thus, as a beginner, your first perspective on cryptocurrency and blockchain technology will greatly influence your investment approach. Don't just look at it as an alternative form of currency, but instead, consider the value of the technology and its role in different sectors of our society, whether economic or otherwise. This will give you not just a broader view of blockchain technology, but also help you become more receptive to innovative ideas and solutions, which could make it easier to identify great opportunities to invest your money like a pro.

Back to our opening statement on controversies—this is something you must always keep at the back of your mind. The cryptocurrency market will never run out of controversies. For every person who hails this market as an exciting opportunity, there'll always be another chiding it as a bubble. The best way to navigate this is through in-depth research. As a rule of thumb, it's good to listen to what people say, but never base your decisions on their opinions. All decisions involving your money must be based on quality research. Otherwise, you might fall victim to herd mentality, and this never ends well.

This book gives you not just beginner-level information on cryptocurrency but useful pointers that can help you navigate the wider blockchain ecosystem as an investor. Therefore, apart from teaching you the foundational knowledge of cryptocurrencies, you can also use it as reference material in the future. It's written in a stepwise manner, from the origins of money and cryptocurrency to a glimpse of what the future holds for cryptocurrencies. This is to help you understand some of the unique challenges we face and how we can use blockchain technology to circumvent or solve them altogether.

Building on that, we will also discuss some useful implementations of blockchain technology that are currently making headlines in global financial markets, particularly through DeFi solutions. This will also give us insight into some of the amazing opportunities beyond the speculative aspect of holding onto cryptocurrencies and hoping to make profits from price appreciation. With DeFi, you actually put your cryptocurrencies to use, delivering greater value than speculating on price increases.

On top of that, we'll also discuss some of the popular myths that have been spread about cryptocurrencies in the past. Myths are common in our society, especially where people don't have the best understanding or knowledge of something. Even the internet had its fair share of myths during its formative years. Most of these have been widely publicized over the years, and some still exist today, despite all the advancements we've had in this sector over the years. This goes to show you that even in a world awash with information and an abundance of reliable resources, misinformation and heresy will always be an obstacle you must overcome, and this is only possible through in-depth research and conducting due diligence before investing your money.

Over time, you'll realize that with the right information, you don't necessarily need to invest in cryptocurrencies for speculative purposes. The high level of price volatility in this market makes it almost impossible to predict how the prices might change from time to time, which means that if speculation is all you have going for you, then you might be in for a rude shock.

It's critically important to understand the economic dynamics of market demand and supply before you invest in any blockchain asset. In simple terms, something is generally perceived to be of great value in the market when more people desire it. Thus, the more people want to get their hands on it, the higher its price will be. The secret is to understand what might be driving the demand for the cryptocurrency. Once you figure out those dynamics, you can have an easier time predicting demand fluctuations and whether to increase your investment or not.

Another important aspect of demand is in the utility value of the cryptocurrency. The idea here is to try and answer one simple question—what's so important about this cryptocurrency? Look at Bitcoin, for example. It was primarily created for use as an alternative currency to the dollars and other forms of fiat currency we use. Thus, it mostly derives its value from use as a medium of exchange and other functions of money that we know of, for example, store of value, standard of deferred payment, and as a unit of account. Without these, the cryptocurrency might virtually be worthless.

Other cryptocurrencies that came up since Bitcoin mostly derived their value from trying to improve on the structure and concept of Bitcoin. Thus, their value depends on whether they actually achieve those goals or not. Take Ethereum, for example, whose native currency is Ether. Ethereum is more than just a cryptocurrency. It is a decentralized blockchain that offers more than just the monetary functions associated with Bitcoin. Its open source technology and smart contract functions enable the development of global payment and digital money solutions and lots of applications that have helped to transform the blockchain ecosystem over the years. It's actually through the Ethereum blockchain that many people realized that there's more to cryptocurrencies and blockchain technology in general than acting as alternative currency. To be precise, most of the work taking place in building the metaverse, dubbed the next stage in the evolution of the internet, involves the Ethereum blockchain. NFTs and DeFi activities are mostly taking place on the Ethereum blockchain. As you can see, the more utility value we can derive from Ethereum, the more people will demand for it, pushing up its value.

Finally, and even though we might not discuss this concept at length in this book, it's important to understand the nature of regulatory frameworks around cryptocurrencies before you invest your money. By design, blockchain projects are meant to be trustless technologies. This means that they are mostly self-regulating through smart contracts and other protocols, ensuring that there's no need for oversight from third parties like governing authorities and administrators. In most cases, this is as far as your protection in any blockchain project goes. We have yet to come up with regulatory standards that can be accepted worldwide. Realizing the difficulty in the legalities of regulating cryptocurrencies and blockchain projects in general among other issues, some countries have taken the drastic measure of banning cryptocurrencies in general, while others speak out strongly against them but haven't been able to ban them.

Even though regulation introduces the aspect of centralization in projects that are meant to be decentralized by design, it's highly likely that we'll see more development on this aspect in the future. If anything, regulation might be the key to unlocking the potential of blockchain technology and encouraging adoption and integration into other sectors of our economy. As things stand, the best you can do to protect your investment at the moment is through deep research and due diligence. With the information in this book, however, you have all you need to set foot in the right direction as far as investing in cryptocurrency is concerned.

Chapter 1: The History of Money and Cryptocurrency

You use coins all the time. They always come in handy when you need some loose change, and also make it easier to buy items in smaller units. As much as we find notes easier to carry around, coins give us the convenience of divisibility, which we might not always get with currency notes. Tracing the origins of money, you realize that, like coins, the problem of divisibility has also persisted throughout the history of trade and finance. In particular, divisibility was a major problem in the barter system.

Barter trade means that you have to exchange a product or service for something that you want. Even though this seemed to work for ages, it had its unique challenges. First, it was highly unlikely that you'd find someone who was willing to accept what you had, and in the exact quantities, for whatever you needed from them, also in the right quantities.

Additionally, it wasn't easy to determine the exact value of the items being traded. Let's say you were willing to exchange your herd of cattle for some furniture, and you found someone who was willing to trade with you. It wasn't easy to determine the exact or acceptable value of cattle and furniture that would make an equitable trade.

These are just some of the problems that plagued the barter system. To overcome them, earlier civilizations came up with coins as an acceptable medium of trade. Coins have been an integral part of finance for centuries. The earliest use of coins in trade and finance can be traced back to between the fifth and sixth centuries BCE, when they were accepted as a payment method.

The Greeks

The Greeks are among the earliest documented civilizations to use coins. Interestingly, modern coins still retain some of the Greek coinage methodologies. The Greek coins had a portrait symbol of sovereignty on one side, and a symbol of nationality on the other. In Athens, for example, some coins featured a little owl, the recognized badge of Athens on one side, and the head of Athena, the protector and goddess of Athens, on the other. Most modern coins still follow the same format, with some variations over the years.

As the Greeks interacted with the rest of the world, so did their influence on culture, trade, and finance. Gradually, Greek coinage spread beyond the Mediterranean, both as currency and as collectibles.

The Turks

Another trip down memory lane takes us to modern-day Turkey, during the ancient Lydian Kingdom of 700 BCE. These coins were made from electrum, a naturally occurring amalgamation of silver and gold. Like the Greeks, the Lydian coins were marked with indents on one side and unique designs on the other, which made them unique compared to other coinage.

Since these coins were used in their natural state, they were available in different sizes and shapes, which made it difficult to come up with a unified design for all coins. For this reason, and to create an element of consistency, the value of these coins was determined by their measured weight.

The Chinese

During the Shang Dynasty (1600-1050 BCE), the Chinese mostly used cowrie shells for trade. Their predecessors, the Zhou Dynasty (1050-221 BCE), paved the way for the use of coins, while the Qin Dynasty (221-206 BCE) created a standardized coin system that would thrive across the Chinese Empire. Subsequent dynasties built on their foundation by creating coin variations according to their needs.

Notably, the early use of coins was limited to activities within the empire capitals. However, coins were widely accepted throughout the empire for fines, salaries, and taxes by the start of the Han Dynasty's (206 BCE - 220 CE) reign.

Ultimately, the evolution of coinage within the Chinese empire led to the creation of gold coins with inscriptions of the Chinese cities on them for uniqueness. Most Chinese coins had a round or square hole through which a string would be tied, making them easier to carry around.

The Romans

By 27 BCE, the Romans had advanced a value-based system for their coins. In this system, the value of a coin was determined by the inscription written on it, instead of its value in measured weight. This system is often considered the earliest introduction of the value-based system we call fiat currency today.

Following this approach, the Romans soon saw fit to reduce the amount of metal used in making coins while at the same time devaluing the metal used to create the coin. For example, while the value of a coin was inscribed on it, a coin made of 80% gold would still be more valuable than one made of 20% gold, even if they were both worth the same inscribed amount.

Kublai Khan's Paper Money

Like coins, currency notes have also come a long way. Paper money can be traced back to the 11th century CE, an invention of the Song Dynasty (960-1279 CE) in China. One of the reasons for the creation of paper money was to make it easier to carry large sums of money, which was cumbersome with coins. It's quite interesting that we still have the same problem today. You can comfortably walk around with a suitcase filled with notes in multiple currencies, whose coin equivalent would probably be a truckload.

Other than the fact that coins held intrinsic value and were difficult to counterfeit, their heaviness, especially when you had a lot of them, made them quite an inconvenience. By the time of the Tang Dynasty (618-907 CE), traders frowned upon the use of coins. For large transactions, they had to deposit their coins with trusted agents, who would then note down the deposit amount on a piece of paper, which acted as a promissory note. The promissory note would be issued in exchange for goods, after which the holder would go to the agent to redeem their coins.

Even though the use of promissory notes simplified transactions, they were not accepted as paper currency. The Song Dynasty realized the need to streamline this process and issued licenses to specific agents to act as deposit shops. People would deposit coins at these shops in exchange for notes. Licensing made it easier to control the flow of money across the empire, and by the 1100s, the dynasty assumed direct control of the money system, creating the first government-backed paper currency. They called it the Jiaozi.

The Song dynasty created factories to print this currency, which would expire every three years. Notably, these currencies were only accepted in specific regions within the empire. Towards the end of their reign, the Song administration created a standardized national currency that was accepted all over the empire. This currency was backed by either gold or silver and was available in multiple denominations. The national currency went on to serve the empire for nine years until the Mongols felled the Song Dynasty in 1279. The Mongols issued their own government-backed paper currency, the chao, a system so unique that it wasn't backed by silver or gold, as was the short-lived Chinese currency.

The great conqueror Genghis Khan's grandson, Kublai Khan, introduced a national paper currency in 1260, which was issued with the same authority and trust that was once used in gold and silver-backed currencies. Select government officials would append their names and official seals to each note, marking the currency as authentic. Since this was basically worthless paper, the need for authenticity was further backed by legislation, such that counterfeiting was punishable by death.

Quite significantly, the death penalty helped impose a sense of authority on the currency. Kublai Khan also achieved an incredible feat that other currencies before that had struggled to achieve—getting people to adopt the currency. Throughout human history, people have generally struggled to accept new forms of money. To inspire confidence in the new currency, Khan made it the mandatory form of payment. The death penalty wasn't just for counterfeiters but also for those who rejected the new currency. Thus, anyone who opted for other forms of payment that had previously thrived in China instead of the national paper currency faced the death penalty. As far as confidence and uptake were concerned, this was the magic stroke that aligned the entire nation to a unified payment system.

What Khan managed to achieve wasn't just getting the entire country to use a unified currency, but a currency that wasn't backed by anything other than the intangible sovereign authority of the state, a concept that has thrived to date.

The Journey to Cryptocurrency

Throughout modern history, the sole authority over money has always rested with the state. This explains why governments address money laundering and counterfeiting with the seriousness they do. When left unchecked, the actions of counterfeiters can flood the economy with an excess supply of money, dragging the country into the dire straits of inflation. Of course, governments must also be held to account for printing money to finance their own projects, as this creates the same issue of inflation.

In the wake of the 2008 financial crisis, Satoshi Nakamoto published the Bitcoin whitepaper, outlining the concept of a new type of currency that, like Kublai Khan's, wasn't backed by anything. But instead of the authority of the state, Bitcoin would be backed by the strength of cryptography.

Bitcoin was born!

Since Bitcoin, many other cryptocurrency projects have sprung up, some successful, others not so much. Regardless of what happens to Bitcoin throughout its lifetime, one thing we can't take away from it is that it ushered in the quest and realization that the idea of new forms of money can be actualized. For a long time, we've operated under the guise that money has probably reached the final point in its evolutionary path. Coins and notes thrived, and still do, even in the age of online money transfers. However, Bitcoin proved that we aren't there yet.

Like most new inventions, Bitcoin isn't 100% perfect. As a result, quite a number of the cryptocurrencies that came up after Bitcoin were established with the objective of stepping up where Bitcoin failed. Skeptics have always questioned what the inherent value of Bitcoin, or any other cryptocurrency for that matter, is. To this, we can also pose the same question about modern notes and coins. How can we know the true worth of the money in our pockets? Currencies get devalued from time to time, just like Bitcoin and other cryptocurrencies. So, at what point does the $10 in your pocket become worthless, or when does it become worth so much more than what is printed on it?

A common discussion that rages online and in other avenues regarding cryptocurrencies, fiat currency, and other digital assets is valuation. As an investor, valuation is an important concept because it determines what your portfolio is worth. Digital assets like cryptocurrencies are a huge and evolving market whose potential hasn't been fully tapped yet. However, one certainty about this market is its disruptive potential.

Our modern financial systems have never been the same since Bitcoin. Some banks might still frown upon them, but rest assured that, behind the scenes, they are looking at ways of getting in on this space. The growing popularity of cryptocurrencies is mostly down to the structure of blockchain technology and its benefits.

Many people use digital assets and cryptocurrency interchangeably, yet this shouldn't be the case. Cryptocurrency is but one example of digital assets. Both terms have become popular in recent times in light of growing activity in the use of blockchain solutions. Digital assets represent anything with unique features that is stored online digitally and has some value. Value in digital assets depends on the owner or holder's utility in the asset. For most digital assets, value is also determined by the exclusivity of use, ownership rights.

Apart from cryptocurrencies like Bitcoin and Ethereum, other items that can be aptly described as digital assets include online documents, logos, audio and video content, blogs, and websites. Other than their content, the value of these digital assets is mostly derived from their copyrights or patents. This explains why plagiarism and piracy are usually treated with contempt.

To understand the value of digital content, imagine waking up to some of your personal documents with privileged information posted on social media. The nature of privilege varies from one person to the next, but you can be certain that having your sensitive information in the wrong hands could be catastrophic. For the purpose of our discussions, we'll limit our scope of digital assets to cryptocurrency and blockchain products.

The cryptocurrency space has grown over the years since the success of Bitcoin. Many cryptocurrencies were actually created in an attempt to bridge the gap between Bitcoin and the traditional financial economy. Others were created to try and capitalize on some of Bitcoin's protocol flaws.

There's more to cryptocurrency than its role as a mode of payment. Many people limit their imagination to this, making it harder to maximize their true potential. For example, if you follow that approach, you can only think of cryptocurrencies as alternatives to fiat currency. On the other hand, we have the Ethereum blockchain, which has championed growth and development in many fields. Instead of limiting yourself, broaden your horizons by looking at digital assets as investment tools.

There are many investment opportunities in the digital asset ecosystem, with more investment tools being created all the time. We face many challenges in the world today, from supply chain management to climate change. Blockchain projects offer tangible solutions to some of these problems, adding more value to the projects. This lends credence to the concept of utility. The more uses you can get from a digital asset, the more valuable it is to you, and in the case of blockchain assets, their value appreciates in exchanges.

Blockchain assets have come a long way, and there's still more room for growth. They've evolved from assets mostly shrouded in mystery or, in some cases, considered the preserve of geeks and computer programming enthusiasts, and are now breaking into mainstream industries. Some of the big name brands that we interact with all the time are investing in blockchain solutions because they've already realized the potential in this ecosystem. Real estate investors are experimenting with smart contracts and other blockchain solutions to streamline their business processes. You can even obtain a loan and receive the cryptocurrency in your wallet thanks to micro-loan services on the blockchain.

As a beginner investor or enthusiast in cryptocurrency and blockchain technology, you are getting in at the right time. You have access to lots of information on present and upcoming projects that can help you make strategic decisions on your investments. You know the potential risks to look for, and the signs that you need to cash out of your investment.

As you can see, blockchain projects offer such diversity in solutions that disrupt some of the basic monetary and contractual functions we are used to. The best thing about it is that we are just getting started.

Chapter 2: Blockchain and Cryptocurrencies

The blockchain is a shared, distributed ledger on which transactions are recorded. You can think of it like a normal business ledger where you record transactions as they happen. While the concept of recording transactions is similar, the methodologies used are quite elaborate and complex. The blockchain is built in a manner that makes it impossible to hack or alter written records. Thus, unlike the traditional ledger system used for accounting purposes, where you can change entries for any number of reasons and basically cheat the system, you can't do that on the blockchain. All transactions recorded on the blockchain are duplicated and shared throughout the network, so every single user on the blockchain has access to the same information all the time.

The simplest definition of cryptocurrency, also known as crypto, is a digital currency. However, you'll soon realize that there's more to cryptocurrencies than money. A good example of this is Ethereum, which we can consider as both a currency and a blockchain. The native currency used within the Ethereum blockchain is known as Ether (ETH). However, as a blockchain, the technology behind Ethereum has been implemented in several sectors, including gaming, finance, advertising, supply chain management, and web browsing. Given this example, instead of digital currency, a safer bet would be to describe cryptocurrency as a digital asset.

It's also evident from the Ethereum example that cryptocurrency is but a drop in the ocean in terms of the functions and capabilities of blockchain technology. Many people mistakenly think all there is to blockchain technology is digital alternatives to the currency system we have used for ages. If anything, we haven't even tapped into its full potential yet.

Bitcoin and Ethereum might be some of the most popular blockchain ecosystems today, but they are not the only ones. An important feature of blockchain technology that stands out from these two ecosystems is growth. Initially, most people were skeptical about them, but over time, people flocked to these ecosystems when they realized their inherent value.

The structure of a blockchain is a growing chain of blocks. The transactions recorded on the blockchain are stored in groups known as blocks. Every block can record information up to the limit of its storage capacity. Once it's maxed out, the block is closed and links to the previous block in the sequence. This linking forms an unending chain of blocks, and that's how we end up with a blockchain.

Blockchain Benefits

Why should you be interested in blockchain technology? What do you gain from blockchain technology, compared to the present systems and technologies we have used for years? Understanding the benefits of blockchain technology helps you realize its unique value proposition, and possible avenues for individual or corporate implementation. Let's briefly discuss some of them below. Remember that this is a largely developing sector, so we can anticipate more developments in the future as blockchain technology goes mainstream.

- **Privacy and Security**

Blockchain technology is famed for privacy and security, purely because of its design. Blockchain transactions feature end-to-end encryption, and they cannot be altered, making it impossible for unauthorized access or any other kind of fraudulent activity.

Blockchain data is distributed across a vast computer network, so it's impossible to conduct a targeted hack. This is a significant change from the usual centralized computer networks we use all the time. In such cases, all you have to do is successfully hack the administrative unit or database, and you'd have access to every device on that network.

Another good thing about blockchain technology is anonymity. Other than encrypting and distributing data fragments across the network, all blockchain data is anonymized in such a manner that you cannot access it without the required permissions. This makes it a great solution for journalists, whistleblowers, and any other entity that requires secrecy.

- **Transparency**

Every node on the blockchain network has access to the same kind of information, with all the privacy and security protocols in check. Since all the blockchain data is immutable, everyone on the blockchain can view the detailed history of a transaction. If you run an entity that disseminates information to a group of users, this would be a good solution to prevent some of the common issues that come up about transparency, especially in account management.

- **Trust**

Trust is always a concern, especially in business transactions. Every party to a transaction usually hopes that the other party honors their obligation. Unfortunately, this doesn't always happen. People change their minds along the way, or the transaction could be influenced by external parties with vested interests. Therefore, as much as we try to conduct business transactions on the principle of utmost good faith, the element of trust is never a sure guarantee, not even where parties are bound by a contract.

Blockchain technology takes away these challenges by creating a trustless network. It takes away the need for reliance on one party's goodwill to honor their obligation. Blockchain transactions are coded in a manner such that entities that have never met can trust one another in a transaction, not because of their commitment to the contract, but because the contract is coded in a way that everyone must honor their obligation, or counter measures are automatically implied.

A good example of this is the use of cryptocurrencies. In normal circumstances, we visit banks for most financial transactions. Banks conduct their due diligence, for example, if you need a loan, to ensure that you can repay it. This process involves other entities like credit bureaus and, if you default on the loan, collections agencies. As much as you are bound by the lending contract and you understand the consequences, people still default for different reasons, and third-parties are involved, which makes the entire process unnecessarily expensive.

Blockchain lending solutions use smart contracts to overcome such challenges. With smart contracts, interest rates are set automatically, as is the repayment schedule. Thus, if you get a loan on the blockchain, your payouts will be automated. In the event of default, the smart contracts immediately liquidate the security deposits. Therefore, there's no need to use collection agents and incur the additional cost.

- **Traceability**

Since blockchain transactions are immutable, you can easily trace the history of a transaction. This can be a good solution to streamline supply chain operations. Walmart, for example, has implemented this approach, making it easier to track products back to their origins. For example, if a customer complains about substandard products, they can trace them back to the producer. This way, they can remove a single producer's products from their shelves until they sort out their issues, instead of removing the entire line of products.

This solution can be used to tackle other problems like counterfeiting and piracy. The audit trail created on the blockchain enables information sharing with customers. It also supports the need for provenance and transparency, restoring trust between customers and businesses.

- **Speed and Cost of Transactions**

Blockchain solutions automate every part of a transaction. Without the manual processes, it's generally faster to complete transactions than using the conventional approaches we've implemented for ages. Take the banking sector, for example. Some transfers take days to complete, especially for cross-border accounts involving multiple currencies. On the blockchain, this can be achieved in minutes.

- **Control**

One of the best things about blockchain technology is that it puts you in control of your data. We live in a world where data is such a precious commodity that every corporate entity tries to get their hands on it. The problem with the information we share with companies is that it's often stored in centralized databases, controlled by an administrator. This makes it easier for hackers to gain access and exploit the data for personal gain.

With blockchain technology, you have complete control over your data. Apart from that, transactions are anonymous, so as much as everyone has access to the public distributed ledger records, it's not easy to identify the person behind the transactions. With these kinds of controls, you can set sharing parameters by choosing which entities you'd like to share your data with, and more importantly, for how long. This is enforceable through smart contracts.

- **Innovative Capacity**

The blockchain ecosystem is still in its infancy stage, so there's so much we still don't know about its full potential. However, individuals and companies alike have since created lots of innovative solutions and integrated them into their platforms. Blockchain technology can be implemented in different industries depending on the kind of problems. For example, blockchain immutability has been implemented in providing solutions for common supply chain problems.

We can also use blockchain technology to solve the problem of counterfeiting. Counterfeits pose multiple challenges in every industry where they exist. For example, people have always faked their resumes and certificates when applying for jobs, or seeking promotions, at the expense of other qualified and honest applicants. Since blockchain information is unchangeable, educational and professional information can be stored on the blockchain, serving as the sole point of verification for any interested entity. Other than getting the truth, you can also access it instantly, instead of sending requests and hoping for timeous responses.

Decentralized Banding

Band protocol in blockchain technology is an open standard for decentralized data management. Band is a standard protocol implemented in data governance and management on the blockchain. It is an accepted standard that developers use for decentralized projects that require reliability and utmost trust in data management.

One of the core features of blockchain technology is the creation of a trustless network. This is commonly implemented through the use of smart contracts. A trustless network means that you don't need to know someone personally or call in favors to complete a transaction, which is usually the case in many institutions outside the blockchain ecosystem.

All blockchain platforms operate under the auspices of trustless computing. However, it's impossible for smart contracts to obtain the relevant data on their own. This is because of the absence of a unique interface where decentralized solutions can obtain the necessary data to furnish smart contracts.

Band protocol is a sophisticated data management solution that addresses the issues of reliability and availability of data. The data feeds are obtained from relevant blockchain communities, creating a blueprint for self-moderation and management of data sources. It is through this process that we end up with reliable and trusted data sources.

By creating a standardized protocol for data governance, banding makes it possible for social scalability in data governance. This means that developers can leverage band protocol to build blockchain solutions on a need basis.

One thing we must understand about band protocol is that it doesn't necessarily regulate how data is used. Instead, it sets guidelines for community-driven data curation and management for their decentralized solutions.

Smart Contracts

Smart contracts are simple, self-executing programs used to implement contracts on the blockchain. Their protocol implements the basic if/when...then statements in computer programming, and runs when certain preset conditions are satisfied. The main benefit of smart contracts is that they create immediacy of outcomes by executing contracts as soon as the parties honor their obligations. This application eliminates the usual contract challenges of time wastage and the use of intermediaries to enforce the contract terms in case one of the parties fails to fulfill their obligation. Without intermediaries, contractual agreements made in this manner are faster and cheaper to complete. After all, only two parties are involved in the contract.

Smart contract code is written on the blockchain, instructing a wide network of computers to initiate specific actions when conditions have been verifiably met. For example, if you use a smart contract to buy a used car, possible terms of the contract might include having the car checked by a mechanic of your choosing, verifying that all the features are as described in the purchase agreement, and so on. Once your mechanic confirms that everything has been done according to the agreement, funds are immediately released to the seller, completing the purchase and transfer of ownership to you. Note that this transaction will be updated on the blockchain as soon as it is completed, so you cannot change it. The results and finer details of the contract will be visible only to the buyer and seller.

Apart from simple transactions, smart contracts can also be used for elaborate agreements that require multiple levels of confirmation before both parties are satisfied. In such instances, you must both agree on how to represent the different confirmation levels on the blockchain, and more importantly, the rules that must be followed to implement the confirmations. For such multiple-step contracts, you must also account for exceptions and other possibilities and outline an acceptable approach for dispute resolution. Once your elaborate framework is ready, you can then program it into the smart contract.

Structurally, smart contracts make the traditional contract experience more efficient by increasing the accuracy and speed with which parties to the contract perform their duties. Contract execution takes place instantly as long as the necessary conditions are met. These are automated digital contracts, so there's no need for tedious paperwork or appending your signature to lots of pages. This also takes away the risk of creating reconciliation errors that's common in manual contract signing and filing.

The absence of third parties in smart contracts highlights the trustless nature of blockchain solutions. All records involved in the transaction are cryptographically encrypted, so there's no risk of either party altering the contract after the fact. Without intermediaries, you also avoid contract delays and other fees that are usually charged by such entities.

Besides, blockchain encryption makes it extremely difficult to hack records already written to the distributed ledger. To even attempt such an activity would involve massive financial and energy resources, which is a disincentive to hackers. Each block on the blockchain is connected to the previous and next block in the sequence.

Therefore, to change a single record, you'd have to change the entire chain of blocks on the blockchain, which is a virtually impossible and pointless attempt.

Blockchain Security

Security has always been a concern in online spaces. There are more cyber attacks today than ever before, and given the amount of money held in cryptocurrency and other blockchain products, it's even more important to understand the kind of security protecting your investments online, or offline, depending on the kind of crypto wallet you use.

Security concerns are not just limited to cryptocurrency or blockchain solutions. It's a common theme whenever a new product or system comes up. As long as your money or data is passed through a system, you'd want to know what kind of safeguards they have in place and what reprieves or solutions are available in the event of a breach.

Even though we can consider blockchain to be a relatively new technology, its impact is growing with individuals and companies exploring various scenarios where it could be integrated into everyday activities. This is how the use of blockchain technology has transcended cryptocurrency. Naturally, integrity and security are the first concerns that come to mind before such integrations.

Big companies buying into new technology always inspire the confidence of the masses in the technology. In the blockchain space, we've seen the likes of FedEx, IBM, and even Walmart embrace blockchain technology by integrating it into some of their business processes. Considering the amount of money in their operations, most users feel reassured and confident in using blockchain technology when such companies buy into the technology.

When we talk about blockchain security, we are mostly looking at the concept of risk management. This is about the frameworks, features, and practices that exist in blockchain networks to reduce or prevent the occurrence of risks like cyberattacks or fraudulent activities.

Blockchain technology is inherently built for structural security in terms of the decentralization features, cryptographic methods, and consensus mechanisms implemented for key tasks on the network. Information blocks are interconnected in a manner that makes them almost impossible to hack. Additionally, the use of consensus mechanisms for validation eliminates individual or administrative bias in verification, thereby eliminating major points of failure in network computing.

Beyond these basic blockchain structures, security levels vary according to the type of blockchain. Besides the general blockchain features and functions, we can further classify blockchain networks as private or public. Each of these classifications comes with unique security features depending on the level of user access and permissions on the network.

Private blockchains, for example, only allow access to known members. This means that user identities are vital in such networks, making them inaccessible to users who lack the right credentials. These are permissioned networks where decisions and transaction verification are made through established rules. Contrary to the basic blockchain tenets, private blockchain networks tend to create an oversight or admin role, with more access controls and a demand for user identities.

On the other hand, public blockchains do not restrict entry or participation but still maintain user anonymity. These blockchain networks have clear mechanisms for consensus and validating transactions. Apart from issuing public keys, user identities are anonymous, and there are no centralized controls like we'd expect in private blockchain networks.

Each of these blockchain networks is suitable for different use cases, which also means considering the security measures inherent to each structure. For regulatory or compliance purposes, a private blockchain network would suffice, the admin role notwithstanding. On the other hand, if your emphasis is on distributed computing, this would be best realized through public blockchain networks.

While blockchain networks might differ in their features and functions, they are all structured around three key security layers. Each of these layers is important in that a security breach in one layer can compromise the other layers.

Layer 1: Tokens and Coins

Before you invest your money in a cryptocurrency project, conduct research to understand the security measures they have in place. Under what protocol was the project created? Note that since there's no government control, investing in a cryptocurrency project means you are assuming all the potential risks related to that protocol.

For example, if someone were to discover and exploit weaknesses in the protocol, your tokens and coins would be at risk, regardless of the type of wallet you use, security measures implemented by your preferred exchange, or any other steps you might have taken to protect your investment.

It's always advisable to research the technical aspects of a project. For example, if a cryptocurrency project is centralized, it could always be exploited from the points of centralization. This is particularly important for projects that use the proof of work (PoW) consensus mechanisms.

PoW has been adversely mentioned over the years in terms of resource consumption. As a result, many projects are shifting to proof of stake (PoS) and other consensus mechanisms that do not necessarily exert as high a drain on resources. Before investing in a project that uses PoS, your attention should be on the origins of the project. Generally, users with higher stakes enjoy higher privileges than those who don't. Try and learn about the distribution of stakes in the project to ensure that no single entity on the network has a stake big enough to influence or compromise the project's consensus mechanism.

Layer 2: Crypto Exchanges

The fact that exchanges handle so many crypto business transactions daily makes their security layers an important concern to investors. When researching crypto exchanges to use for your transactions, one of the issues you consider is their security history. Have they ever been hacked before? If so, how did they resolve the matter?

An interesting feature of crypto exchanges that most people never realize is that their security protocols are often independent of blockchain technology. At best, exchanges are nothing more than central web services deployed in data centers or through a cloud service. This realization highlights the value of credibility and trust to investors.

Many blockchain breaches in the past have been executed by exploiting flaws in the security protocols of different exchanges. When you choose an exchange, you trust that they have appropriate measures in place to safeguard your interests. Many exchanges today have sprung up to try and cash in on the cryptocurrency hype. Unfortunately, not all of them invested strategically in securing their platforms. With that in mind, if someone were to successfully exploit the exchange and steal your tokens or coins, there isn't much you can do to recover them. This is also why some exchanges these days have insurance covers to protect their customers in the event of such eventualities, but even so, the insurance cover can only protect you up to a certain limit, so there's no guarantee that you will be indemnified to the full value of your exploited account.

Layer 3: Wallet Security

The final security layer is on you, the investor. We will dive into the finer details of crypto wallets in Chapter 6. However, it's important to understand that, unlike the typical wallet that holds your money, the crypto wallet holds your private and public keys. You can choose between a hot or cold wallet, but depending on your immediate needs, a careful mix of both wallets is a better solution.

You've probably read so much about the security features built into cryptocurrencies and why they are a safer alternative to fiat currency. While this might be the case, these security features are not guaranteed where the fundamental principles of blockchain technology are not fully implemented or where the project infrastructure isn't built on the blockchain.

In retrospect, this casts a shadow over the concept of hot wallets, crypto exchanges, and mining pools because, as much as they have made it easier for investors and traders to engage and transact cryptocurrencies, they were not inherently blockchain protocol constructs. On top of that, you'll also realize that many blockchain projects aren't fully decentralized, while some have critical flaws in implementing the concept of decentralization.

At the end of the day, your money is at stake. Therefore, take the necessary steps to understand the security measures implemented in a project before you invest your money in it.

Is it All Hype?

The technologies we discussed above are real and practical. From time to time, discussions come up questioning the legitimacy and sustainability of blockchain technology. This is a normal experience with new technologies and could also explain why some myths about blockchain technology and cryptocurrency spread like wildfire. Naturally, new technologies always get mixed reactions from users. While some people recognize their utility value and invest their money right away, others are more skeptical and won't spend their time on it.

We also have those who are ever indifferent, probably listen to both sides of the discussion but never make a move, or when they do, they proceed with extra caution. For example, there are people who believe in the traditional regulated banking system so strongly that they cannot consider putting their money into a new disruptive mechanism that lacks government regulation. To such individuals, cryptocurrency and blockchain technology are nothing but a scam, or at best a bubble that will burst soon.

While you can understand their concerns, especially from all the stories online about people losing money in cryptocurrency scams, hacks, and so on, none of this is hype. Blockchain technology and cryptocurrencies are a reality. In fact, many governments have realized their potential and the impact they could have on society in the future with the right infrastructure and are trying to come up with applicable legislation to regulate this sector. With proper regulatory protocols in place, it might be easier to fully take blockchain solutions mainstream, especially into the financial markets.

We are talking about a future where blockchain technology is fully integrated into the traditional financial system, where you can go to your bank and trade in cryptocurrencies the same way you conduct normal transactions. This will be a reality, but the challenge is how to make it happen. Remember that banking, for example, is a heavily regulated and controlled industry, as are other aspects of the financial sector. On the other hand, blockchain technology was designed to break away from these controls as an autonomous system that self-regulates.

If there's one lesson we've learned throughout the history of humanity, it's that nothing is impossible. If we put our minds to it, nothing can stop an idea whose time has come. Blockchain technology is one such idea. While still in the infancy stage, there are crucial developments going on in the wider ecosystem, and as more people find utility in it, you get the feeling that we are not so far away from legislation that will bring some level of regulation in this space, and usher in what we might rightly consider the next phase of the financial revolution.

Chapter 3: Traditional Banking vs. DeFi

The primary goal of decentralized finance (DeFi) is to use blockchain technology to streamline the financial services sector by enabling businesses and customers access to the usual financial services they do, but with the benefits of blockchain technology. This means that, through DeFi, you should be able to access deposits, loans, interest, and other kinds of payments. Thus, the course of DeFi isn't to act as an alternative in the way cryptocurrencies like Bitcoin have been framed, but to streamline, or in some cases, change the way we access financial services. You can think of DeFi as a unique infrastructure for accessing financial products and services, leveraging blockchain features like smart contracts, which is a key component of the Ethereum blockchain.

Smart contracts are unique, self-executing contracts used on blockchain projects. These contracts are codified in a manner such that as long as the terms of the contract are met, the terms of the contract are automatically executed. There's no need to follow up on either of the contractual partners to honor their end of the contract, so no third parties will be involved.

Smart contracts are the foundation of DeFi. Other than holding cryptocurrencies, they allow users to interact on the blockchain under specific rules outlined in the contract. This is how DeFi transactions among users are conducted. In this case, smart contracts somewhat assume the transactional role of brokers and banks, and in the process, create a trustless network where users can conduct peer-to-peer transactions such as making payments, lending, investments, and any other kind of financial transaction.

But, why is there a need to democratize the traditional concept of finance? Fiance has thrived for centuries under a centralized setup, where gatekeepers and other governing authorities exercise control over the market. Because of this setup, almost every transaction or interaction involves a financial third party, creating unnecessary costs and making financial transactions expensive. Think about it for a moment; almost every transaction you've ever conducted at the bank was loaded with unnecessary transaction costs. From purchasing or selling stocks and bonds to obtaining a loan or mortgage for your house, the list of transaction costs is mind-boggling.

As currently constituted, the structure of the centralized financial system makes it impossible to bypass third parties. For example, if you wish to trade in the stock market, you cannot avoid the stock brokerage costs. It's as simple as that—you must pay to play.

This is where DeFi comes in. In a nutshell, the premise of DeFi is to eliminate or reduce the hold that third parties have on customers or the market in general. With peer-to-peer transactions, everyday users have more control over the activities in the market.

DeFi empowers everyday users to take on and efficiently manage some of the tasks that are usually handled by third parties like banks and brokerages, for example, trading, lending, and borrowing.

Let's put this into perspective with some simple calculations. You deposit money into your savings account, and your account earns 0.5% interest on that amount at the end of the year. On the other hand, the bank lends this money to another customer at an interest rate of 5%. Depending on the customer's credit score, the rate might even be higher. Just like that, the bank has made a 4.5% profit from your money. It gets even worse when this customer might be yourself.

With DeFi, you lend directly to other customers. Therefore, instead of depositing your money into the bank, you can keep it in your wallet, and when you lend it to someone for 5%, you earn the full profit, not some bank that uses your money.

While this concept is exciting, we must also note that centralized financial systems still have a role to play in DeFi. This is why we used the words "eliminate" or "reduce" when describing the premise of DeFi. In the real sense, it's almost impossible to completely eliminate banks and other third parties from the financial system. Our financial systems were built around these institutions, so it's highly unlikely that they will go away. For example, you'll still need to link your cryptocurrency wallet to your bank account to obtain the dollars you convert to cryptocurrency and trade on blockchain platforms. What we can look forward to, however, is a seamless integration between DeFi and centralized financial systems, where customers can enjoy the best of both worlds.

Utility in DeFi

Let's start by answering a common question that comes up from time to time—is Bitcoin DeFi?

Well, Bitcoin allows you more control over your money in that you can own it, store it, receive it, or send it to someone anywhere in the world without a trusted intermediary like a bank. So, in a way, we can think of Bitcoin as one of the earliest applications of DeFi. But, we know that the DeFi concept is primarily built on the Ethereum blockchain. What Ethereum has achieved so far is to build on the gains of Bitcoin and advance the promise beyond the cryptocurrency concept, hence the emergence and success of concepts like DeFi and NFTs.

One key aspect of DeFi is that it allows us to create and use programmable currency. This feature makes it easier to combine the benefits of blockchain technology, particularly security and control, with the normal services offered by financial institutions. This makes it easier to load more transactional activities on cryptocurrencies like payment scheduling and investments, which wouldn't normally be possible with Bitcoin, or cryptocurrencies in their role as money.

In terms of utility value, there are many products and services offered in the traditional financial market that can seamlessly fit into the DeFi model. The best thing about it is that the list of services keeps growing by the day, as more people realize the inherent value of DeFi. Let's have a look at some of the ways in which you can implement DeFi today:

Transactional Value

This is purely about sending and receiving money from anywhere in the world. Coming off the success of Bitcoin, the Ethereum blockchain was built to enable users to send and receive money all over the world in a secure manner. Conducting these transactions is as simple as sending a text message or an email. All you need is the recipient's public address and you'll instantly send them cryptocurrency from your digital wallet. Most of these transactions are completed in minutes.

As a rule of thumb, it's always safer to work with the major exchanges for your transactions. This is important because, from experience, they are generally more secure than new or upcoming exchanges. Having been around for a while, it's also likely that they have better customer support services, in case you ever run into problems with your transactions.

You can also use DeFi for conversion purposes, which will help you move money from your digital wallet into your bank account. Note that this conversion can take anywhere between an hour and a few days, depending on the security measures your bank has in place and the exchange platform you are using. Either way, this is still much faster and cheaper than the processes we go through to send money to someone in a different country.

Money Streaming

We live in a world so obsessed with real-time events that users demand everything from news reporting and sports broadcasting to NASA's voyages into space be presented in real-time. No one wants to miss out on an important moment. Well, DeFi allows us to do just that, earn money in real-time. The concept of money streaming means that you can now receive money on a circumstantial basis. For example, instead of earning your salary at the end of the month, you can structure your salary and earn it for every second or minute of your employment. This automated process has potential in subscription-based products, allowing users to pay for products or services as they are consumed, instead of a flat fee.

For example, let's say you pay $50 for internet at home every month, yet you spend most of your time in the office. With this approach, you might only end up paying for what you consume, reducing your average monthly internet expenditure.

Stable Currency Access

If you've watched the Bitcoin market for a while, you're aware of the fact that it's a market that's quite volatile. Prices rise and fall randomly, and in many cases, the difference can be quite steep over a short period of time. This kind of volatility makes investing in cryptocurrencies quite a risky venture. With this in mind, investing in financial products based on cryptocurrencies can be a problem. A potential DeFi solution for this is the use of stablecoins.

A stablecoin is a type of cryptocurrency whose market value is pegged to something else: for example, fiat currency, another cryptocurrency, or even commodities. Their main function is to support transactions on crypto exchanges. For example, instead of exchanging your dollars for Bitcoin, you could exchange them for a stablecoin, and then use the stablecoin to buy another cryptocurrency.

Since stablecoins derive their value from external factors, their values are relatively stable, making them suitable for retail transactions on financial products. Their stability also makes it easier to protect investments or savings from high volatility in the market.

Lending and Borrowing

Lending and borrowing are two of the most important financial transactions that take place every minute in global finance. From retail to institutional customers, there's always an entity in need of some money and another willing to provide it at a cost. Through DeFi, borrowers and lenders can both have their needs met by exchanging crypto assets.

There are two approaches to lending and borrowing on DeFi, pool-based or peer-to-peer financing. Pool-based financing is where lenders create a pool of resources from which borrowers can get the funds they need at a fee. Peer-to-peer financing, on the other hand, is where users request financing directly from specific lenders. Note that in the case of pool-based financing, creating a pool of resources generally involves establishing a third-party to manage the pool of funds.

As an individual lender, DeFi makes it easier to profit from your crypto assets. For long-term investments, there's the potential for earning high interest rates. The beauty of DeFi is that anyone can use the platform to earn a passive income.

Even though DeFi introduces a new dynamic to lending and borrowing, some of the traditional aspects of this market remain unchanged. One of these is the borrower's creditworthiness. Lenders usually assess the borrower's profile to determine whether they can actually repay the loan, and on time.

DeFi upholds this concept, but without either party to the transaction having to explicitly identify themselves. In this case, the borrower deposits collateral, which is automatically transferred to the lender in case they default on the loan. Collateral can be fronted in different forms, including NFTs. Using this approach, borrowers and lenders don't necessarily need to share private information or go through credit checks to ascertain the borrower's creditworthiness.

Usher in Global Trade

One of the game-changing features of DeFi is that it opens up global avenues for business. In the traditional financial system, access to global business sources is pretty much restricted to a few traders, usually those who have massive financial muscle. Investing in DeFi solutions means that you can access financial services from anywhere in the world.

Let's say you want to borrow some money. You'll be able to borrow from anywhere in the world. You are no longer restricted to borrowing from specific institutions. The beauty of accessing financial products from such vast sources is that it enhances competition, giving you access to better rates and terms of business. This is unlike the usual banking situation where you are forced to take whatever rates the banks decide to push down your throat.

Token Exchanges

The Ethereum blockchain is home to hundreds, if not thousands, of different crypto tokens. Through decentralized exchanges (DEXs), you can easily trade different types of tokens without ceding control of your digital assets. The conventional financial version of this is changing your currency for another when you visit a foreign country. The main difference is that, while traditional exchanges operate within fixed schedules, DeFi exchanges are always open. The best thing about it is that you can always be certain that someone somewhere in the world will be willing to trade with you.

Advanced Trading Tools

While some investors are only interested in buying and selling through DeFi products, others need solutions that give them more control over their trade activities. In this category, we have traders who use features like limit orders or margins on their trades. These tools give investors an edge over those whose aim is simply to buy and sell.

In a global market that's always open for business, such tools help you refine your trading activities such that you can now trade with the same level of finesse that a professional financial advisor or broker uses in the traditional financial market for investments like options trading, bonds, and stocks.

Given these benefits, you can also use the fund management products available on the Ethereum blockchain to manage and grow your portfolio. One good thing about this is that you don't need someone to manage your portfolio at a cost, so you don't lose a portion of your profits to transaction and professional management costs.

Crowdfunding

The Ethereum blockchain is great for crowdfunding and other allied ideas. This is based on the blockchain concept of peer-to-peer interactions. When people come together, they can achieve great things. If you have a brilliant idea but lack the financial muscle to see it through, the Ethereum blockchain is one good place to seek financing. You have access to potential financiers from all over the world.

The crowdfunding process is transparent and straightforward, so your financiers can see how much they have raised towards the amount you need. It's also possible to track how the funds were utilized in your project, which is good for accountability. Furthermore, your financiers can also set deadlines for automatic refunds such that they get their money back if your project hasn't met certain requirements within a set timeframe.

Insurance Products

The traditional insurance market is often plagued with inefficiencies at different points, from payouts to a lack of transparency in the contracts. This is why many people have a difficult time getting their claims processed. Through DeFi, you have access to a new range of insurance products that can be paid out faster, are more affordable, and, because of the automation in smart contracts, come with transparent and straightforward terms.

All this is possible because the kind of data used to process your claims isn't shrouded in mystery, as is usually the case with many insurance providers. Besides, through decentralized insurance services, clients who would normally be priced out of traditional insurance now have better, affordable solutions.

Pros and Cons

The flurry of activity in the cryptocurrency market lends credence to the unending discussion of whether or not they could be a fitting alternative to the conventional financial system. Indeed, while we consider how far the traditional financial sector has come, and its position in the global economy, it's almost unfathomable to imagine it being completely wiped out by cryptocurrency. Perhaps, seamless integration of the two systems seems a more feasible concept than complete obliteration. To understand this proposition, let's review some of the pros and cons of each alternative:

Traditional Finance: The Challenges

- **Inclusivity**

One of the best ways to see the potential of DeFi is to understand the problems that exist in our financial system. Inclusivity, for example, is a problem that has plagued the financial sector for years. If you have a bank account and can enjoy most financial services, it might be a surprise to learn that not everyone has the same rights and privileges. Millions of people all over the world are either unbanked or underbanked, unable to enjoy things like ATM services, online banking, or even basic access to a savings account.

It's also quite sad that, in some cases, the inability to access financial services might even make someone an undesirable candidate for a potential employer. Many employers conduct background checks before engaging candidates. Without a bank account in your name, you might not have a credit score, which could deter an employer from considering your application. Remember that employers receive hundreds, or even thousands, of applications all the time. To sift through all of them in fine detail might be unnecessary hard work, so instead, they can filter the applications according to different metrics. If one of these eliminates applicants whose financial information isn't complete, you might easily miss out on an opportunity.

- **Account Limitations**

One of the common problems in banking is the fact that your account could be limited or blocked for any number of reasons, all at the discretion of the bank. From time to time, you'll hear people complain about their accounts being blocked or limited, and having to go through a torrid time to get the limitations lifted. Many have had their accounts blocked permanently, losing their money in the process, with no help forthcoming from the legal authorities either.

Apart from user accounts, central banking organizations or even governments can exercise their authority and close down financial markets and institutions at will, which creates a huge problem for investors. A government can always exercise its administrative mandate and terminate these operations despite the possible outcry from retail and institutional clients.

- **Data Privacy Concerns**

When onboarding new customers, banks collect a lot of personal information, which is often held in central databases. While this information is useful to the bank for different purposes, it also creates a lot of challenges for banks, which have often been exploited by hackers and other entities for illegal purposes.

The worst thing about it is that while you share your personal information with financial institutions to create an account and enjoy their financial services, you sign away some rights to how that information will be used. Financial institutions have different kinds of contractual arrangements with other third parties like their IT service providers, credit reporting agencies, and so on, who can all access this information without your direct consent.

- **Time Constraints**

Naturally, banks and other financial institutions have limited trading hours. If you need their services, you must align your business or needs with their hours. This is preposterous, particularly in a world that is embracing 24-hour economies. It can be quite frustrating to run a 24-hour business yet you cannot access your bank with the same convenience.

Another concern in this regard is time zones. Many businesses have embraced technology and, where possible, opened up their operations to the rest of the world through e-commerce. Unfortunately, banks do not offer the same convenience. The most you can enjoy is online banking through their mobile apps and websites, but these only offer a limited range of services. If you need banking services that demand your physical presence in a different country, you'd have to factor in the time zone and adjust your schedule accordingly.

There's also the time inconvenience where you have to wait one or two business days, or even longer, to complete bank transactions. This is usually an unpleasant experience especially when you don't have the luxury of time on your side. For example, if you made the transaction on a Friday, it might only be confirmed very late on Tuesday the following week, yet perhaps you needed the transaction completed urgently.

- **Cost of Banking**

Banks are essentially brokers. They charge a fee to facilitate your transactions or administer and manage your accounts. Their brokerage role is, in fact, one of the reasons why banks can also be a nuisance. There are different types of fees that banks usually charge, and unfortunately, some of them might be unknown to their customers. This is why you hear people talk about hidden costs and charges.

Some of the common banking charges include the cost of using ATMs, wire transfers, online transactions, overdrafts, minimum account balances, account opening, and account maintenance fees. Generally, fees are often an annoyance, whether they are listed upfront or they sneak up on you, as many hidden fees do. They eat into your profits or savings and make your purchases and other transactions more expensive.

Well, bank fees exist for one simple reason—banks are in the business of making money. Their bottom line is to make money by any means necessary. The dollars or cents they charge on your account might seem insignificant, but when they collect that amount on millions of accounts, they make a tidy profit. Yet, all this happens at your expense.

It gets even worse in instances where your transaction with the bank must involve another party. For example, when mortgaging a house, the closing costs usually include fees levied by attorneys, homeowners associations, credit reporting agencies, and insurers, which cumulatively make your transaction more expensive.

DeFi: The Benefits

Granted, it might take years for DeFi to attain the level of monetary value associated with the traditional financial market. However, we must also appreciate the fact that DeFi has been on a steady, sustained growth trajectory since its inception, which is proof that people find tangible value in the products and services offered. Let's have a look at some of the benefits of investing in DeFi solutions below:

- **Breaking Down Barriers**

By design, DeFi solutions are built to address most of the core challenges that plague the traditional financial systems by virtue of centralization. Banks and other financial institutions have always been prime targets for attacks because of the value of information in their databases. Depending on the attacker's intentions, some of this information might be worth more than the amount of money held in the banks.

Another barrier that is directly addressed by DeFi solutions is intermediaries. By eliminating or significantly reducing the role of intermediaries, DeFi solutions make transactions more affordable and easier to complete.

DeFi solutions also address the issue of inclusivity by making financial services accessible to users who would have been locked out of the traditional financial system. Improving access is great for the economy because it brings more money into circulation. At the same time, DeFi also creates new categories of investment opportunities, providing users with additional income streams and more alternatives to diversify their investment portfolios.

- **Management Costs**

DeFi eases the pressure on financial institutions and customers by taking away common cost centers like data storage, auditing, financial oversight, and so on. Since the blockchain is immutable, it becomes the single source of truth for everyone, thereby reducing or even eliminating some management costs often associated with the traditional financial sector. Manipulating records on the blockchain is practically impossible. Thus, DeFi solutions provide a security assurance and guarantee of integrity when conducting financial transactions.

- **Transparency**

Compared to traditional financial systems, the aspect of decentralization provides transparency in financial transactions as the distributed ledger ensures that everyone on the blockchain has access to the financial activities taking place. Besides, through the unique cryptographic methods applied, information on financial transactions is only documented after authentication.

This is a bold step in enhancing due diligence when conducting financial transactions. One area where this could be useful is in detecting and avoiding financial scams, which are quite common and sophisticated in the traditional financial sector. The same applies to unfair business practices, where unsuspecting customers are often lured into traps by hidden clauses in contracts.

By implementing smart contracts, clients are certain that once they complete their end of the contract, the other party will automatically complete theirs. Besides, the way records are kept on the blockchain makes it easier to identify all aspects of a change made to a transaction, including the time, the person who made the changes, the nature, and the impact of the changes. This goes a long way towards enhancing the integrity of the financial products being offered.

- **Revamping the Lending Business**

DeFi solutions have breathed a new lease of life into lending solutions. This is one area where the elimination of third parties plays well into the hands of end-users by getting rid of unnecessary costs. DeFi links the borrower and the financier, reducing the cost and the duration involved in confirming the transactions.

Through smart contracts, there's no need for banks and other intermediaries that are often charged with ensuring verification and other terms of the lending contract. Thus, DeFi offers automatic safeguards to all the parties to the lending contract.

- **Interest on Savings**

Just like a normal bank account, you can earn interest on your crypto assets through specific DeFi products. A good example of this is Compound, an interest rate protocol that has driven growth in the DeFi market by allowing users to lock their cryptocurrencies in smart contracts. With hundreds of millions of dollars locked in Compound, it is one of the key drivers of growth in the DeFi sector, encouraging a savings culture and earning interest on the savings.

This is also a good point to introduce yield farming, a process where users commit idle cryptocurrencies for use in lending protocols and earn interest on them. Other than helping holders earn passive income through interest, yield farming also helps to bring more crypto assets into circulation instead of lying idle in user wallets.

- **Tokenization**

Through the robust functions of smart contracts, issuing tokens on the Ethereum blockchain has opened up the blockchain to other industries by creating digital assets, for example, in the real estate sector. In real estate, tokens are often used to create fractional ownership of physical properties. This concept is similar to buying fractional stocks using online trading platforms like Robinhood.

Granted, many people are priced out of the traditional real estate market. You'd normally need a few hundred thousand dollars to own property. Without that kind of money, your only option is to get a loan for the property, which leaves you in debt for a long time. With tokens, you can buy fractional ownership of a property. This is great, especially for commercial property, as you'll earn income from its commercial proceeds.

DeFi: The Potential Challenges

Even though DeFi is quite promising, it's fair to look at the potential pitfalls so that, as an investor, you go in with an open mind. Just like every other investment in the traditional financial market, DeFi solutions are not risk-free. Learning about the potential challenges gives you better insight into DeFi and how to estimate its true potential. Let's discuss some of these challenges below:

- **Complexity**

While DeFi solutions are presented as exciting alternatives to financial products in the traditional money markets, investing isn't as simple as walking to the bank. For beginners, it can be quite confusing, particularly in light of the number of applications and investment avenues available. Apart from that, the process of moving money from your bank account through an exchange and into a noncustodial wallet can also be intimidating to beginners.

- **Uncertainty**

DeFi solutions are a new approach to finance, and like most new solutions, the element of uncertainty always lingers around. Millions of users all over the world have invested in these solutions. At the same time, many others are skeptical of the uncertain nature of these products.

It's not easy to convince people to invest their money in a new financial model, an alternative to the traditional financial system that has existed and thrived for centuries. It gets even worse when you consider the kind of volatility and uncertainty experienced in the blockchain markets; case in point, Bitcoin.

DeFi projects are enslaved to their native technologies. Thus, the project naturally inherits the problems and risks inherent to the technology behind it. If the hosting blockchain is unstable, the project will inherit the same flaws, which is risky for investors.

- **Risk of Theft and Scams**

Fraudsters are aware of the potential in DeFi, and will always try to lure new investors into scam projects. Most of these are presented with exciting yields that practically outshine what you'd get from traditional financial investments. As a rule of thumb, always exercise caution when the yield is too good to be true, because it almost always is.

Other than scammers, we also have hackers who try to exploit weaknesses in different dApps in the market. If successful, you might lose your investment, yet the prospect of recourse comes down to whether the developers can or will compensate you.

- **Cost Consideration**

DeFi and blockchain solutions are generally considered cheaper than the alternatives provided by traditional financial markets. This, however, might not always be true. Gas fees required for smart contracts could increase depending on the number of processes involved in a transaction. The fact that gas fees can also fluctuate depending on the level of activity on the blockchain can see a transaction cost hundreds of dollars in gas fees.

- **Market Volatility**

Volatility is one of the biggest challenges for anyone trading in cryptocurrencies. Prices fluctuate all the time, such that you could easily lose the traditional financial market equivalent of a year's yield, or even higher, overnight in your crypto portfolio. This is a common reason why many people are still jittery about investing in cryptocurrencies or blockchain products like DeFi solutions.

- **Abandoned Projects**

There's always a possibility of the project being abandoned, as developers move on to other things. In such cases, the logic written into the project might still execute as created, but the project will never receive additional upgrades, effectively leaving it to die a natural death.

- **Liquidity Risk**

Even though the DeFi market is growing, the total liquidity held in the market is nowhere near the value of the traditional financial sector. Remember that this is pitting a market that is a few years old against one that has existed for centuries. For context, there are individuals whose net worth is greater than the liquidity value of the entire DeFi market.

- **Accountability**

When you invest in DeFi solutions, you are fully responsible for your actions, and misdeeds. This is something many people are not aware of. The project developers are not accountable for mistakes on your end. For example, if your account is exploited because you set weak security parameters, you are on your own. This is in stark contrast to the responsibility measures put in place in the traditional financial sector, where you can report to authorities, or raise an alarm over suspicious activity on your accounts, and have someone look into it.

The most that DeFi projects do is eliminate intermediaries in financial transactions, while you are fully accountable and responsible for your assets and funds. There are simply no checks and balances in place to prevent loss from human error or mistakes. This, therefore, means that other than investing your money, you also need to learn about the technologies powering the DeFi solutions, so that you understand the ins and outs of them, their potential vulnerabilities, and how to protect yourself against them.

Ultimately, the prospects of DeFi solutions come down to a balance between solving the real problems in the traditional financial system and the world at large, like climate change, and deriving utility value from the projects. This creates the element of sustainability in the projects and makes it easier and more feasible for people to invest, which speeds up mainstream acceptance and adoption.

The Environmental Impact

While the advancements in distributed ledger technologies have been promising so far, there's one loophole that sends jitters down the spine—their environmental impact. This comes down to mining. In blockchain terms, mining is a validation process through which new crypto assets are created. This process consumes a lot of energy, in some cases, more than the annual average that some countries use.

But, why is it important?

The mining process involves different consensus mechanisms. A consensus mechanism is a fault-tolerant process that ensures the legitimacy of all the nodes and transactions on a blockchain network. This is also how the blockchain remains so robust that it's prohibitively expensive or impossible for someone to hack the entire blockchain.

The biggest blockchain projects, Bitcoin and Ethereum, both use the proof of work (PoW) consensus mechanism, though Ethereum is expected to switch to Proof of Stake (PoS) soon. Proof of Stake, on paper, is supposed to require less energy consumption compared to proof of work, but until this is implemented, the most we can do is speculate. Besides, it is within the Ethereum blockchain that most of the blockchain projects that have made headlines in recent years are built, notably DeFi, NFTs, and even the futuristic metaverse. As these projects go mainstream, there's a good chance that more users will find tangible value in them, increasing the demand. Thus, the most we can do about Ethereum's switch to PoS is to speculate on the energy-saver status until full implementation.

Proof of Work is one of the most resource-intensive consensus mechanisms in the blockchain realm. While it's not easy to give a direct and accurate estimate of the amount of energy consumed through these processes, reliable estimates suggest that the annual consumption might be higher than what Argentina or the Netherlands consume in a year, yet these are countries with industrial processes that directly contribute to their annual income.

Generally, the average annual energy consumption by blockchain projects is expected to increase in the future with increased adoption and integration into different industries. One reason why energy consumption is increasing is the competitive nature of blockchain projects. Mining blockchain assets is competitive in that users are more incentivized to mine the next block when the potential reward is higher. Unfortunately, blockchain assets are energy-intensive by design, not fault. This lends credence to the concept of deterring attempts by a single entity to take over and control the entire network.

Ultimately, it is a classic example of a necessary evil. On one hand, mining blockchain assets exerts a toll on our non-renewable sources of energy, making them bad for the environment. On the other hand, this consumption is what bolsters the network, supporting the concept of decentralization and maintaining network security.

Integration and Future Prospects

From our discussions above, it's clear to see that both traditional finance and DeFi are useful in different kinds of financial transactions. If anything, individuals and entities who use traditional financial models could still benefit from DeFi. It's fair to say that at some point, these two systems will integrate seamlessly to meet the evolving needs of users all over the world.

The important question as we look to the future is how this integration can be implemented. One thing we can be certain about is that DeFi, as it presently exists, cannot fully replace the traditional financial system. DeFi transactions are conducted in blockchain markets, which have their own unique strengths and weaknesses compared to the traditional financial markets. The main point of confluence at the moment is that before lenders can issue funds on a DeFi platform, they must have the fiat currency converted to the acceptable tokens or crypto coins on the respective DeFi platforms.

Indeed, traditional finance has held the global economy together for years and will continue to do so in the foreseeable future. However, at the same time, as blockchain platforms and services become mainstream, we'll see more people coming to terms with DeFi. With this knowledge, we can anticipate further uptake in DeFi solutions, particularly in light of the inherent benefits we discussed earlier. Whether DeFi can replace traditional finance is a matter of speculation, but one thing that we can be certain of is that at some point in the future, the two financial models will coexist. Compared to traditional finance, DeFi eliminates or greatly reduces most of the institutional or bureaucratic bottlenecks involved in transactions. Thus, anyone can use DeFi solutions at any given time.

Most people who are either locked out of the traditional financial system or cannot access some services for any number of reasons will definitely be attracted to the promise of DeFi. For instance, those who are unable to get financing because of credit score concerns will find a worthy reprieve in DeFi. On the same note, DeFi also creates new opportunities for earning passive income, making it a worthy consideration for both retail and corporate investors.

Following in the footsteps of blockchain products and cryptocurrency, in particular, there will be various claims about DeFi that you cannot afford to take at face value. Cryptocurrencies like Bitcoin, for example, have often been touted as the new frontier, poised to wipe out fiat currency. The reality at the moment is that, at best, we can talk about Bitcoin or cryptocurrency's potential. Complete obliteration of the fiat system is near-impossible, despite the significant benefits of digital currency.

We can apply the same concept to DeFi. Indeed, DeFi has the potential to disrupt the traditional financial sector. We talk about eliminating middlemen and the costs thereof, but the reality is that this thesis might not hold 100%. For example, users must still access different exchanges to trade their digital currencies, which charge some fees for their transactions. Clearly, the role of a middleman still exists.

What we can be certain of is that, with a higher prevalence among users, traditional financial institutions like banks will have to find a way to get in on the action. Away from their transactional mandate, banks offer a sense of security and stability. This comes from the regulatory frameworks and legislation by which they are bound. Therefore, users who might be skeptical about digital assets could find it easier to change their stance when a bank starts issuing DeFi solutions. This is borne from the belief that regulation in the banking sector gives them certain legal protections in the event of any mishaps with their transactions.

The future is about integration. Many banks are increasingly tapping into blockchain technology in different capacities to explore the utility value therein and how to offer value-added services to their customers. Therefore, while we cannot say that the traditional financial system is unshakable, we also cannot give a blanket assessment that financial institutions will be pressured into aligning with future trends and fully adopting DeFi solutions. Instead, we can be certain of accelerated acceptance and integration of DeFi into traditional banking.

Mostly for relevance and the need to remain competitive in a cut-throat industry, innovative banks will come up with unique DeFi products tailored to meet unique customer needs. Even so, there's the conundrum that's legislation and regulation which they still have to circumvent. So far, regulating or establishing astute legislation around blockchain assets has not been easy. Traditional banking institutions that might be willing to go the extra mile will have to contend with the potential complications that might arise from this initiative.

In particular, full-scale integration of DeFi into traditional banking systems would require, at the very least, revising most of the conventional structures and processes that have held the global banking system in place for years. This also means that financial institutions would have to embrace additional risks while still grappling with the inherent risks within the industry. Regulation also means that financial institutions might need additional approvals on top of what we have in place at the moment.

The bottom line is that complete integration is still some way into the future. Presently, however, DeFi is quite promising for investors. Once you understand the basics of trading cryptocurrencies, there's no reason why you shouldn't take the step up to DeFi. The yields so far are attractive, but that shouldn't blind you to the potential risks. Study the market well to understand how certain factors affect yields and the general performance of the DeFi sector. More importantly, pay close attention to events in the Bitcoin market, because most blockchain assets generally feel the trickle-down effects of significant action in the Bitcoin market.

Chapter 4: Crypto Myths

The biggest blockchain project, Bitcoin, is always in the news for different reasons. Financial analysts and enthusiasts all over the world are keen on events in the Bitcoin market for different reasons. As an investor in cryptocurrency, it's normal to pay attention to events in this market too, seeing that the changes could have a significant impact on your investment.

Blockchain investments are a new and exciting opportunity. The problem is that many people don't understand what they are about, and this creates a lot of room for misinformation. This is a common feature of human psychology. As long as we don't fully understand how something works or what it's about, people will always come up with different versions to try and explain it, hence the foundation of myths.

Even though cryptocurrencies have been around for years compared to the traditional financial market, this sector is still in its infancy stage. Some experts contend that what we have explored so far is but a fraction of the potential of blockchain technology, yet we are already on the cusp of building the next phase in the evolution of the internet, through the metaverse. Given the unknowns, it's almost natural that myths and half-truths will spread online about cryptocurrencies. Let's have a brief discussion about some of the common myths and debunk them with facts.

The Crypto Bubble

This is obvious. People always expect the new kid on the block to fail. Many cryptocurrency projects have actually failed. However, each of those projects failed for different reasons unique to their ecosystem. Casting our gaze on Bitcoin and Ethereum, it's understandable why people would be concerned about the bubble bursting, especially when you consider the level of volatility in this market.

To debunk this myth, we need to understand the dynamics of economic bubbles. An economic bubble arises when there's an unsustainable increase in the market value. In such cases, the price keeps rising, mostly out of speculation, yet there's no growth in the fundamental value of the asset. Eventually, the price rises to a point where it cannot match the inherent value of the asset.

Notably, most people invest in Bitcoin for speculative reasons. Since its inception, Bitcoin prices have fluctuated through multiple cycles, yet they always recover and stabilize over a defined range. In economics, we can see that Bitcoin goes through the normal economic cycles of booms and busts, as have many other investments in the past. This is a young market, so even though it's not prudent to conclude the existence or legitimacy of a bubble, the fluctuations in this market are characteristically normal enough to suggest that Bitcoin is here for the long run. Considering the influence Bitcoin and Ethereum have on the wider cryptocurrency market, we can say the same about the market too.

The Cryptocurrency Fad

That cryptocurrencies are a fad that will die a natural death is a claim you'll come across online all the time. This is mostly peddled by people who believe that cryptocurrencies will never replace traditional financial models. What such arguments fail to realize is that even though cryptocurrencies were modeled as alternatives to fiat currency, they don't necessarily have to replace the old model. Instead, they can coexist.

There's so much potential in blockchain technology for it to be a fad. Many industries are already realizing the significant benefits of integrating blockchain technology into their operations. In particular, the features of immutability and decentralization have made operations easier, faster, and more affordable where seamless integration has been achieved.

Still, on the subject of fads, it's not lost on us that email, the internet, and even computers were once considered fads that would only appeal to computer nerds and enthusiasts. Today, a day without them is almost unfathomable.

As in the case of whether cryptocurrencies are a bubble or not, we cannot reliably predict what will become of the cryptocurrency market in the future. However, given the growing interest, adoption, and implementation in mainstream sectors of the economy, we can expect further development in the cryptocurrency sector as blockchain products are refined to enhance their practicality.

Interest isn't just from individual users; we have financial institutions and governments considering how to implement cryptocurrency solutions in projects. This, however, will greatly depend on figuring out a way to stabilize the prices or establish some level of control over the volatility.

Replacing Fiat Currency

Fiat currency has existed for centuries. It's highly improbable that they could be completely replaced by cryptocurrency, a model that is only a few years old. When someone tries to convince you that cryptocurrency will replace fiat currency, take a moment and think about the advancements in the history of money and everything we have gone through to get to this point to realize how far-fetched an idea that is.

Cryptocurrency or any other proposal must first gain massive acceptance in that people understand it and are willing to use it as currency. The fact that we are still debunking myths about cryptocurrency is reason enough to believe that it has not attained the level of acceptability to replace fiat currency.

The best we can achieve with cryptocurrency at the moment is integration into the modern financial systems, such that they can be accepted concurrently with fiat currency but not as a direct replacement. In theory, direct replacement might be possible, but in practice, we are still years away from that even becoming a reality. For example, El Salvador took a bold step towards cryptocurrency acceptance by recognizing Bitcoin as legal tender. While this move has had its benefits, it has also had its fair share of problems, to the point that the IMF implored El Salvador to rethink this strategy.

We have to understand one important thing about fiat currency that makes it difficult to be replaced by cryptocurrency—control, and the necessity of it. Imagine the kind of turmoil that economies would experience if they held a significant portion of their finances in cryptocurrency, say, for example, Bitcoin. As volatile as the market is, the value of a country's resources could be wiped out in a few hours. While we might decry the challenges of centralized economics, this is one area where we must appreciate its importance. Control allows governments to oversee taxation, fund crucial infrastructure projects, and other social programs that millions depend on.

Assuming that we manage to replace fiat currency with cryptocurrency, the meltdown that we've experienced in the Bitcoin price upheavals would be experienced on a massive scale in every country. Inflation and many other economic challenges that we face today would be experienced at exponential levels. Without monetary policies to control inflation, governments would struggle to deal with economic pressures like unemployment.

Insecurity Concerns

Cryptocurrency is a new concept, as is the blockchain technology that powers it. It's normal, in such cases, for people to express concern about security. Indeed, when you invest a lot of money in cryptocurrency, it's only fair to get some guarantees of security.

One possible reason for the insecurity myth is the principle of decentralization. Coming from a financial world of rigid controls and regulation, it's easy to see why some people would peddle such a myth. Traditionally, our money is held by banks, and there are clear guidelines on their functions and roles as custodians of our money. Should anything go awry, you also have protocols on how to report the bank to the regulatory authorities, and so on.

In comes blockchain technology, whose first bold move is to sound out banks and other intermediaries in the financial sector that their days are numbered. Instead of banks, all information on financial transactions is written on the blockchain and, for transparency, accessible to everyone on that blockchain.

The consensus mechanisms used in blockchain projects are meant to make it impossible to change any information once it's been written to the blockchain. Therefore, your cryptocurrency is safe. Perhaps the form of insecurity you should be concerned about is human error and mistakes, particularly in how you store your crypto assets.

There are lots of safeguards you can implement to protect your cryptocurrency. For example, using cold storage facilities instead of keeping your digital assets in exchange-managed wallets. In a general sense, cryptocurrencies are secure. We just need to embrace the fact that things are changing, and changes tend to make establishments uncomfortable.

For context, many computer scientists, enthusiasts, and security experts have reviewed Bitcoin's open-source code, yet it has never been hacked. Most of the myths about insecurity actually stem from third-party enterprises that use Bitcoin, which might have been compromised for different reasons, but Bitcoin itself has never been hacked. More often, third parties are compromised because of flawed or insufficient security approaches or data breaches. Since it was created in 2009, the core protocols behind Bitcoin have run securely with an impressive 99.9% uptime. This is also partly due to decentralization. The blockchain nodes are spread across networks in more than 100 countries, so no single entity can gain enough capacity to disrupt the system, not even a government, for the simple reason that there's no single point of failure.

Environmental Concerns

For a long time, Bitcoin and other cryptocurrencies that use the Proof of Work (PoW) consensus mechanism have been accused of being bad for the environment. Indeed, mining such assets is an energy-intensive process. However, it has become apparent over the years that it's not easy to determine the actual environmental impact of mining, or to distinguish it from other features of the digital economy.

For example, we have fully embraced e-commerce, and the global digital economy is thriving for that reason. However, no one talks about the environmental impact of the digital economy. A few million people in the world can access Bitcoin and other cryptocurrencies. Compare this with the billions who are plugged into the digital economy through smartphones, laptops, tablets, and other gadgets, and we have ourselves an energy conundrum.

Let's take another example, the global financial system. Think about the ATM machines, bank branch networks, buildings, company cars, and so on. All of these affect the environment in some way. They are more advanced and have a wider reach than Bitcoin, and they have also been around much longer. Surely, their cumulative impact on the environment over the years is greater than the fabled impact of cryptocurrency.

Let's not even get started on the energy impact of gold mining, seeing that the gold standard is the monetary policy upon which currencies derive their value. According to this policy, the value of money is preserved by a hard asset, like gold. When governments issue a currency, the value inherent in that currency depends on the amount of gold the government has in its reserves. This also explains the push by many countries to increase their gold reserves.

Therefore, while we cannot convincingly refute the fact that Bitcoin and cryptocurrencies in general exert a toll on global energy resources, it's also time we considered the possibility that the magnitude of these claims has possibly been exaggerated in favor of the status quo, whose impact is just as damaging, if not worse.

Besides, the environmental impact will mostly depend on the energy sources in use and their drain on the power grid. For example, if you are using fossil-power to mine cryptocurrency, the immediate impact on the environment is increased carbon pollution. On the other hand, if you are using sustainable sources of energy, your impact on the environment should be considerably lower.

We also take note of the fact that cryptocurrencies are in their infancy stage, and are still evolving. Even at this stage, conversations about energy consumption have yielded positive responses from the blockchain communities. Ethereum, for example, is moving from Proof of Work to Proof of Stake, a consensus algorithm that significantly reduces its impact on the environment.

Empowering Illegal Activities

This aspect of crypto is, perhaps, the result of watching too many movies. You've probably watched a fair number of movies where criminals use cryptocurrencies for payment. The myth around this is that, in the real world, cryptocurrencies are a haven for criminals. Indeed, it is true that some criminal elements have devised innovative blockchain solutions for their operations. However, that doesn't make cryptocurrency a preserve for criminals. It's the same way we know that some well-run criminal organizations maintain bank accounts whose identities cannot be easily tied to their criminal undertakings.

The fact is that all forms of money, throughout the history of mankind, have proven just as useful to criminals as they are to you and me. It's therefore impossible to discriminate about whether one entity should benefit from money more than another. The point of money is to keep it in circulation, which is great for the economy.

As a store of value, medium of exchange, and for other functions of money, criminals use cryptocurrency just like you do. However, one area where criminals might actually engage in nefarious activities is by operating a scam blockchain project. Such projects are usually created with legal or legitimate intentions, aimed at luring unsuspecting investors. In this case, you innocently invest in a blockchain project after reading its prospects in the whitepaper, researching online, and in your due diligence, believing that you are making a sound investment. Unfortunately, you end up investing in an elaborately executed heist.

As soon as the criminals behind the project reach their goals, they fold the project and disappear with your money. Now, this all sounds scary, but the interesting thing about most of these scams is that they usually share the same approach—promising incredibly high yields. Indeed, volatility in the cryptocurrency market might make some of the yields possible, but the unpredictability of the markets means it's impossible to offer such returns with 100% certainty.

That being said, authorities have upped their game, and through anti-money laundering (AML) and know your customer (KYC) initiatives, a global crackdown on the use of cryptocurrencies for criminal activities has forced many criminals out of the game.

Besides, in the unlikely event that a scam is successful, people usually draw a lot of lessons in its wake, which act as useful learning points on what to be on the lookout for in the future.

No Utility in the Real World

Some critics unfairly push the narrative that cryptocurrencies, and in particular, Bitcoin, do not have any tangible value in the real world, and where useful, it's only for funding illegal activities. We have already addressed the second part of that claim in the previous point. The claim about a lack of utility value isn't true either.

First, you must understand that Bitcoin is both a currency and a blockchain platform, and for each of these functions, it is useful in different instances. As a blockchain, Bitcoin is a useful development platform. Just like the Ethereum blockchain, it is a platform where developers can create innovative products based on the blockchain fundamentals of decentralization and immutability.

Bitcoin is also the foundation of many other cryptocurrencies, in that they came about as Bitcoin forks. This means their projects came into existence by improving one or more features of Bitcoin, but their source code borrows heavily from the Bitcoin source code.

You are also aware of Bitcoin's use as an alternative to fiat currency, which is, perhaps, one of its most notable roles so far. You can use Bitcoin to pay for stuff online, or even in physical stores that accept Bitcoin as a mode of payment. Many institutional investors hold onto Bitcoin to hedge against inflation, in a similar capacity as gold.

Going even further, governments all over the world are actively looking for ways of bringing regulation into this space. This is because they understand that there's so much potential in Bitcoin and the entire cryptocurrency ecosystem, and with proper protocols in place, they could spur innovation in different sectors of the economy.

What we must understand about value is that people perceive value differently. For example, when Bitcoin was launched in 2009, its value was almost nothing. Yet, in 2021, it traded as high as $69,000 per coin. Value is all about perception. This also explains the age-old adage "one man's meat is another man's poison". Let's explain this with the Ethereum blockchain.

The native currency of the Ethereum blockchain, Ether (ETH) doesn't have the dollar value that Bitcoin enjoys in the market. However, it derives value from the utility of the

Ethereum blockchain. Ethereum is the foundation of decentralized finance, non-fungible tokens, and many other innovative blockchain projects you will interact with. As far as the digital asset economy is concerned, Ethereum is like Amazon. It plays host to almost every type of digital asset you can think of, and this is also how it creates utility. Today, many investors realize the incredible value of cryptocurrencies in investment, finance, venture capital, and application in other sectors of the economy, hence the growing desire to own them.

Gambling Away Your Money

Here's another interesting take on cryptocurrency—that you are gambling your money away. Proponents of this myth often gleefully cite the volatile nature of Bitcoin to back up their allegations. It's no secret that Bitcoin's volatility is unlike many assets in the financial world. However, it's also unfair to compare the young and upcoming Bitcoin market with financial markets that have enjoyed decades of growth and stability.

The cryptocurrency market is at a crucial stage where governments all over the world are working on robust regulatory structures to protect the interests of investors. This is quite promising, as has been evidenced by hedge funds and companies like Tesla throwing their weight behind cryptocurrencies.

Where does gambling come in? Well, most people who buy cryptocurrencies are speculative investors. They buy, hoping to profit from soaring prices in the future. There's no guarantee that the prices will rise or the timeline within which this might be possible. Thus, even as you hold onto dear hope, the odds might be stacked against you, just like in gambling, where the house always wins.

However, what sets this market apart from gambling is that, as it matures, we realize more value in blockchain projects beyond speculating on what may or may not happen. As more blockchain projects go mainstream, the trajectory of this market soars upwards. Despite the obscene level of volatility in the market, value in the market is more apparent today than it was some years back. Innovative investors have even started using traditional financial approaches like the dollar-cost averaging method when acquiring cryptocurrencies at different points to strategically streamline their potential for returns.

Compared to the 2017 boom, Bitcoin's volatility has gradually declined over the years. This, in part, is due to the entrance of institutional investors into the market. The financial muscle of institutional investors plays a big role in pushing the idea of a project going mainstream. This also increases confidence in the market, such that when the prices fall, fewer people panic and try to cash out. Instead, many investors hold on, and some even use this opportunity to acquire more crypto assets at a discount.

The rule of thumb when dealing with investments like Bitcoin that are quite volatile is to always conduct your due diligence and invest wisely, lest you make beginner-level mistakes and liken the entire market to gambling.

Overtaking Bitcoin

The premise of this myth is that there will be a blockchain project bigger and more successful than Bitcoin. Well, we cannot predict what will happen in the future, but one certainty is that Bitcoin's position in the evolution of blockchain technology will forever be unchanged. To be precise, Bitcoin isn't the first cryptocurrency to exist; it is the first one that succeeded in delivering the promise of digital money, backed by fundamental blockchain features like decentralization.

Many cryptocurrency projects have come up as Bitcoin forks, attempting to fix or improve on some of the flaws in the Bitcoin protocol, and try to overtake Bitcoin in the process. However, none have achieved anything that gets them remotely close to Bitcoin's influence, let alone overtaking it.

Bitcoin remains not just the most popular cryptocurrency, but of all the thousands created over the years, also the most valuable by a long shot. The success of Bitcoin is such that it features in the same league as some of the top companies by market capitalization listed in the S&P 500. We are talking about companies like Amazon, Apple Inc., Johnson & Johnson, NVIDIA, and Tesla.

Bitcoin makes up more than half of the total cryptocurrency market, not to mention lots of other crypto projects that are forks of Bitcoin. On top of that, Bitcoin has stayed true to its original mission statement, an open and decentralized currency. This, and the first-mover advantage, puts Bitcoin in a strong position to stay ahead for the foreseeable future.

For any upgrade to the Bitcoin protocol, 51% of the global community must agree and support the idea. This concept has helped Bitcoin evolve and adapt to the changes and demands of its users over time, making it both relevant and timely.

It is possible that in the future, another cryptocurrency might arise and strongly rival Bitcoin. However, given the kind of headway Bitcoin is making and its progress in terms of integration into different sectors of our economy, it's hard to see how that becomes a reality, at least not anytime soon.

Chapter 5: Exchange Platforms

Imagine walking to your bank and buying the crypto you need. Better yet, sign into your bank's online account and transfer some crypto from your account to another, or use it to pay for your monthly Netflix subscription. This all sounds great, and maybe in the future, it will be possible. However, at the moment, you can't do it directly. The only way that could be possible is if we had clear regulations and guidelines in place that banks and customers could follow to conduct such transactions. Without those, your only option is a crypto exchange.

Crypto exchanges are platforms where cryptocurrency transactions take place. They support the exchange of cryptocurrencies for other cryptocurrencies, fiat currencies, and digital assets. They basically work like the exchanges we are used to, such as stock exchanges and forex exchanges. Like these exchanges, crypto exchanges assume the role of intermediaries between buyers and sellers, therefore earning transaction fees and commissions.

Choosing the Right Exchange

There are two types of exchanges—centralized and decentralized. Centralized exchanges are controlled by a recognized entity, like a company. They act as intermediaries between crypto buyers and sellers and, because of their structure, are considered the more reliable option compared to decentralized exchanges. Centralized exchanges are responsible for most of the transactions taking place in the blockchain ecosystem.

Decentralized exchanges are structured for peer-to-peer transactions. As such, there's no need for an intermediary. As they are the exact opposite of centralized exchanges, some traders believe they abide by the true blueprint of blockchain technology, hence prefer them over centralized exchanges. Notably, decentralized exchanges don't support the exchange of cryptocurrencies for fiat currency.

Naturally, users of either exchange can cite various reasons why they favor one type over the other. However, the most important thing is to understand that no single exchange will ever be perfect for everyone across the board. When selecting an ideal exchange, you should always prioritize your personal needs and interests, then look for an exchange whose technical capability meets your requirements. Here are some pointers to guide you on how to choose the most suitable exchange for your needs:

- **Security**

Cryptocurrencies do not enjoy the same level of protection that traditional investments like stocks and bonds or your money in the bank do. Thus, before you invest in any exchange, find out what additional protections they have for you in case things go awry.

Even though some exchanges like Gemini and Coinbase bank the dollar account balances in bank accounts insured by the Federal Deposit Insurance Corporation (FDIC), your cryptocurrency balances don't enjoy the same protection. To this end, some exchanges purchase insurance policies to protect their customers, while others have various security measures in place to protect their users.

The security of your assets is something you should never take lightly. Given the amount of wealth held in exchanges, hackers and other criminal entities are always looking for a way to compromise their systems. Remember that exchanges are at the center of all blockchain trading activities that involve buyers and sellers. Therefore, as the network grows and more people start using blockchain solutions, their inherent value grows, and hackers are even more motivated to pursue exploits.

- **Availability**

Your preferred exchange might be unavailable to you because of your location. This is often because of national or state regulations. In countries like China and Egypt, cryptocurrencies and exchanges are banned. It's important, therefore, to review the existing legislation in your jurisdiction to understand whether you can access exchanges without contravening the law. You can learn about an exchange's limitations and the legislative confines of their operation in their terms of service or on their websites.

- **Fees**

Exchanges make money from transaction fees and commissions. Since they're getting something from each of your transactions, it's wise to understand just how much they are taking, and whether it's a sizable sum to deter you from using their platform again.

By default, exchanges that are relatively easier to use tend to be more expensive than the complex ones. This, perhaps, is because they assume the responsibility for all the technical stuff, so all you have to do is sign in and conduct your business. With this in mind, you might want to reconsider ditching an exchange because its fees are relatively higher than most.

The secret is to figure out why the exchange charges what it does and what their direct competitors are offering. Even though some exchanges have a fixed charge to use their platforms, most exchanges charge a percentage of the value of your transaction. You'll also find exchanges whose charges fluctuate according to the level of price volatility in the market. The bottom line is that exchanges implement different pricing mechanisms, so your best move is to evaluate the value you get from their services against the fees charged.

- **Trade Volume**

The trade volume in an exchange can make it easier or more difficult to complete your transactions. Trade volume represents market liquidity. A high volume increases the chances that you can buy or sell your crypto assets whenever you want to, because there'll always be lots of interested buyers and sellers. In terms of liquidity, the more popular exchanges generally have higher trade volumes, so you have a better chance of completing trades on these exchanges than the relatively unknown or smaller ones.

Trade volume is also an important consideration because it determines whether you can complete transactions at a good price. By now you are aware of the level of price volatility in the cryptocurrency market, so it's in your best interest to find an exchange where your trades can be completed as fast as possible. If it takes longer to complete transactions on an exchange, it's highly likely that your asset might have lost value due to volatility. It's also possible that you might benefit from volatile swings in your favor, but in the investment business, it's always prudent to plan for the worst.

- **Coin Variety**

Variety is another factor you should consider when selecting an exchange. Even though there are thousands of cryptocurrencies and many others are still being created, you won't find all of them offered on every exchange. Popular cryptocurrencies like Bitcoin, Ethereum, and Litecoin are available on all exchanges. However, if you seek newer or relatively unpopular cryptocurrencies like meme coins, you'll probably have to research further to find exchanges that don't just list them but have sufficient trade volumes to warrant a valid investment.

An important point to note about unique cryptocurrencies like meme coins and other altcoins is that most of these are highly risky investments, even riskier than investing in established assets like Bitcoin.

- **Taxation**

Taxes aren't the easiest feature of finance to figure out. Many people struggle to understand the basic tax regimes that apply to their incomes. Taxing cryptocurrencies is even more complicated, especially because of the absence of explicit legislation to govern and regulate that sector. So far, tax implications on blockchain assets are still evolving, which makes it even harder to figure out how to file your tax returns on crypto assets.

One of the taxation targets for investment purposes is usually capital gains tax. This is a tax on the profit earned when you sell an asset. For example, if you buy Bitcoins at $25,000 and sell them at $30,000, capital gains tax will be charged on the $5,000 profit earned. It's easier to track gains and losses if you restrict your trades to one exchange. However, most people use multiple exchanges, so it's difficult to reconcile all trade activities for tax reporting purposes.

The most important thing about taxing crypto assets is to research and find out the applicable legislation where you live, so that you don't run into trouble with the authorities as a tax cheat.

Ultimately, the choice of exchange comes down to your personal preferences and investment objectives. Everything else is subjective. As your preferences and investment objectives evolve, so will the appeal of different exchanges to your overall investment goals. When it comes to trading crypto, the most useful weapon you have is research. Always strive to learn as much as you can about the assets and exchanges before investing your money in wildly volatile markets and investments.

Exchange Security

The volume of transactions processed by exchanges is always an incentive for cyber criminals to try and exploit them. As there are different exchanges in the market catering to different user needs, you must research their security protocols first, and only invest once you feel confident that your money will be safe passing through their hands. Either way, there's still no ironclad guarantee of security since even the oldest and most established exchanges in the market are always targeted. Here are some methods you can implement to secure your exchange account:

- **Hot and Cold Wallet Combination**

As we've mentioned separately in this book, you are safer using both hot and cold wallets, particularly with multi-signature security. The last thing you'd want to do is have all your coins stored in one wallet. In the event of a breach, you stand a high chance of losing everything.

- **Two-Factor Authentication (2FA)**

Two-factor authentication is a hot trend in digital security—not just cryptocurrencies, but almost every other mobile application or website that handles sensitive user data has implemented this additional security layer. While passwords offer some level of protection, hackers can use sophisticated gadgets and strategies to try and exploit them. A common way of doing this is through phishing websites, visiting unsafe websites, or downloading malicious programs that install keylogging code on your devices.

Even though a hacker might have your password, they'll still need to physically access your phone, for example, to retrieve the two-factor authentication code. This is how two-factor authentication protects your accounts beyond the use of a password. You can also use an authenticator service like Google Authenticator that generates one-time login codes that expire within a short time.

- **Prompt Updates**

Exchanges generally send you an email as soon as a transaction has taken place on your account. You will receive alerts when a withdrawal or deposit is made against your crypto address. Beyond sending you these updates, some exchanges provide more functionality within the email message, allowing you to cancel the transaction or close the account if you did not authorize the transaction.

One of the first things hackers do when they gain access to your account is change some of your identification information, like phone numbers, email addresses, or mailing address. To protect your account from such incidents, some crypto exchanges block your account from making withdrawals for a few days or weeks after updating your personal account information or settings.

Convenience in Crypto Exchanges

Crypto exchanges bridge the gap between traders and investors just like normal stock exchanges do, despite the absence of a centralized governance authority. Cryptocurrencies have come a long way, and those who have traded in them since 2009 can relate to the fact that, apart from creating a platform for buyers and sellers, exchanges offer one of the most important things for any investor—convenience.

If you have ever traded stocks or any other financial instrument through brokers or banks, you have probably encountered some unfortunate limitations that might even lock you out of investing in some stocks. Since one of the reasons behind cryptocurrency was to eliminate some or all of the institutional bottlenecks in the traditional financial system, it follows that crypto exchanges also build on that foundation.

Perhaps one of the biggest beneficiaries of exchange convenience is the retail investor. In this category, we have individual investors and small scale investors. These are investors who generally spend small amounts of money on their trades. Traditional exchanges, in contrast, tend to favor institutional investors because they move large sums of money in transactions, earning the exchanges more in commissions and other account-related services.

- **Fractional Investment**

As a beginner crypto investor, you'll certainly appreciate being able to purchase fractional values of your desired cryptocurrency. For example, most people rush to buy Bitcoin. However, the price of a single Bitcoin is prohibitive for the majority of new investors. Instead of buying the whole coin, you can buy a fraction of the cryptocurrency depending on what you can afford. Therefore, if you only wish to buy a portion of a Bitcoin worth $1,000, you can do it through an exchange. The beauty of this feature is that you can use it to create a balanced investment portfolio with various cryptocurrencies without blowing your investment budget.

- **Open Markets**

Crypto exchanges are always open, so you can buy and sell whenever you want to. The only potential hindrance you might encounter is heavy traffic on the blockchain, making it impossible to complete the transactions as intended. This might also result in the exchange website being down or too slow to process transactions at the speed you are used to.

Other than the instances when the market is backed up, access to a market that's open throughout gives you the benefit of trading whenever you are prepared. In a way, it also means that all investors across the world have access to the same information and can act on it whenever they see fit. Your trading activities are not limited to market trading hours, as is the case in the traditional investment markets. Interestingly enough, traditional investment markets generally allow institutional traders and investors access to the market before they open to the public and after they close to the public.

- **Order Transparency**

It's always wise to study the market and understand the trade volumes, especially when coupled with research and information in the media and other reliable outlets. This can help you gauge the market sentiment towards a cryptocurrency before committing your money.

Thanks to blockchain transparency, you can view order books for different exchanges to establish how a certain currency has been traded in the market on that day, week, or month. This information is useful, especially before you place a large order.

- **Prompt Trade Settling**

Crypto exchanges allow you to settle your buy or sell activities as soon as the blockchain network allows. This way, you don't run the risk of your trade losing value while waiting for it to settle. This is a common challenge in the traditional investment markets, where it might take even two days to settle some transactions. In a market that allows institutional traders access before opening and after closing hours, they are always at an advantage over individual traders, especially heading into the weekends or public holidays. Crypto exchanges are open throughout, so you don't have to worry about those challenges.

Creating An Exchange Account

Having covered some of the conveniences of using exchange accounts, let's go through the simple steps you can follow to open an exchange account:

- **Select an Exchange**

First, you must choose a crypto exchange. There are several exchanges around, each catering to unique user needs. Read about some of the major exchanges in the market; their pros and cons, user reviews, and more importantly, whether they have ever been hacked before, and how they handled the matter.

Some of the factors you should consider when comparing different exchanges include their customer support services, fees and commissions charged, reliability, and reputation.

- **Account Creation**

This is a straightforward step once you settle on an exchange that meets your trading and investment needs. You will provide the personal identification data required by that exchange. The exchange will then verify this data, and once complete, your account will be ready.

- **Funding Your Account**

Sign into the account with your user credentials. You will find different alternatives to depositing money into the account. Most people link their bank accounts because it's easier to move money between the account and the exchange account.

As a rule of thumb, always take the highest security measures within your control. For example, do not link your main bank account to your exchange. Opening a bank account takes minutes, so open one specifically for crypto trading. You can always transfer the amount of money you need for trading from your primary account into the bank account linked to your exchange account.

- **Buying Crypto**

With the required amount in your account, you can now buy the cryptocurrencies you want. The speed of completion will depend on the amount of traffic on the blockchain, but most transactions are completed in minutes.

- **Transfer to your Wallet**

Finally, you can leave the coins in your exchange account if you still intend to conduct other transactions with them. However, if you are done for the day and won't need to use them for a while, it's safer to move them into your wallet.

Note that as long as the coins are in the exchange account, anything could happen to them. Besides, some exchanges hold both your private and public keys, so in essence, they own your coins. To avoid any unforeseen risks, transfer the coins to your wallet right away.

With the information above, let's quickly review some good examples of crypto exchanges that can give you an easier time as a beginner. Even as we review the exchanges, remember that this information is only accurate as at the moment this book was published. The crypto market is quite volatile and disruptive, so there might be a few changes in the exchange market after the date of this publication.

Before you choose any crypto exchange, consider all the factors we've discussed in this book, plus your personal investment goals, to settle on a platform that guarantees you the best value for your money. Having considered factors like platform security, payment methods available, fees and commissions, and the types of crypto assets accepted on the platform, below are the suitable exchange platforms for beginners:

- Recommended exchange for beginners: Coinbase (also ideal for Bitcoin trades)

- Best exchange for lowest fees: Abra

- Best exchange for security: Gemini

- Recommended decentralized exchange: Bisq

Ultimately, remember that whichever of these exchanges you choose, they are not regulated by any government authority. For that matter, there's no guarantee that your investment through any of these exchanges will be protected. If anything, you could lose some or all of your money.

Even though the crypto market is growing tremendously, it is a speculative and highly volatile market. If you are ever unsure of anything, consult a professional before you commit your money. Choosing the right exchange platform is like choosing the right vehicle—you must carefully consider your options before settling on one that will not just meet your needs but is also economical and can serve you for a long time.

Government Restrictions

As much as the crypto market has experienced tremendous growth since Bitcoin in 2009, it has, from time to time, been a haven for criminals and other nefarious entities that have rubbed authorities the wrong way. The issue of decentralization, coupled with the absence of regulation, means that governments cannot directly have a hand in the large pool of money that exchanges hands all the time. This also means that governments miss out on taxes.

Authorities in different countries have been exploring the possibility of instilling a sense of order into this market. For example, El Salvador became the first country to recognize Bitcoin as legal tender. This move was met with widespread skepticism and criticism from various governments and organizations, particularly the IMF.

Locally, state and federal administrations have been exploring possible avenues to bring sanity and control to this market. Notably, cryptocurrency is not considered legal tender in the United States. However, this doesn't take anything away from the fact that cryptocurrencies are becoming more popular over time. In response, different states have varying regulations in place, depending on their assessment of the crypto value chain and the potential legalities involved in the transactions.

Remember that even though cryptocurrency is not legal tender in the U.S., the IRS considers it a valid representation of value. This means that, where applicable, the IRS could come after you for failing to disclose gains from trading cryptocurrencies. That being said, the tax aspect of cryptocurrency is still a conundrum for many people, so it's always wise to consult a professional if you are ever in doubt.

The United States Securities and Exchange Commission's (SEC) view is that cryptocurrencies are securities and can be traded as such. Therefore, the laws that apply to normal exchanges like the stock market and forex markets equally apply to crypto exchanges. On the same note, the SEC actively monitors crypto exchanges and their wallets.

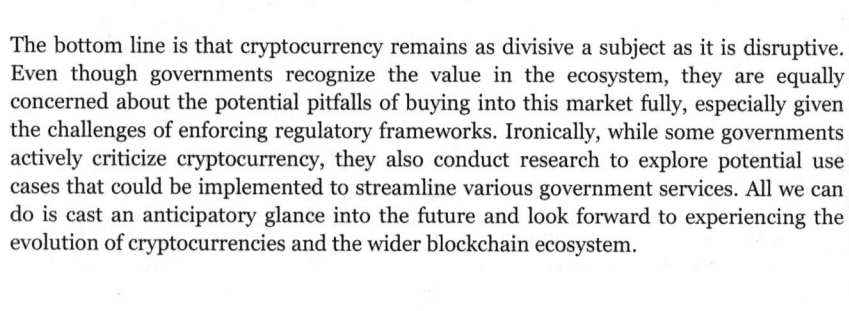

The bottom line is that cryptocurrency remains as divisive a subject as it is disruptive. Even though governments recognize the value in the ecosystem, they are equally concerned about the potential pitfalls of buying into this market fully, especially given the challenges of enforcing regulatory frameworks. Ironically, while some governments actively criticize cryptocurrency, they also conduct research to explore potential use cases that could be implemented to streamline various government services. All we can do is cast an anticipatory glance into the future and look forward to experiencing the evolution of cryptocurrencies and the wider blockchain ecosystem.

Chapter 6: Wallets

Crypto wallets are platforms or solutions used to store private and public keys while at the same time offering a convenient interface for managing our crypto portfolio. It's through these functions that you are able to transfer crypto assets on the blockchain. In the previous chapter, we mentioned the role of exchanges in creating marketplaces where traders can interact and trade in blockchain assets and fiat currency. Wallets are integral to exchange operations because they act as your bank account.

While crypto wallets offer custodial services like a bank account, the difference is that they don't actually store your crypto assets. They only store the keys you need to access and conduct business with your assets. All your crypto assets are always live on the blockchain. Without the keys, however, no one can access them.

In the blockchain ecosystem, keys are quite important because they prove authenticity and help with validation. If you ever lose your keys, you won't be able to access your crypto assets. We can also use the role of keys to shed more light on the nature of transactions on the blockchain. For example, we send or receive cryptocurrency tokens from time to time. However, what most people don't realize is that there's no sending or receiving taking place. Instead, what happens is that your private keys are used to sign and authenticate transactions.

This further supports our earlier statement that your crypto assets are always live on the blockchain. Once your private keys authenticate a transaction, it is broadcast to the blockchain, and the blockchain updates the account balances in your account and the recipient's.

Thus, since crypto wallets don't store your currency, their relationship with your account balances is to read the public blockchain ledger and update balances according to valid and completed transactions. This is also part of the transparency benefit of blockchain technology, where everyone has access to real-time information on all transactions on the blockchain.

Private and public keys are long strings of random alphanumeric characters that are virtually impossible to predict. This is one of the reasons behind the assurance of security on the blockchain. Public keys can be shared with anyone. They are like your bank account or delivery address. People use it to send you money. Your private key, on the other hand, is a secret, like your password.

Public and private keys are paired such that even though someone can initiate a transaction with you through your public key, that information will come encrypted and can only be decrypted with your private key. Thus, you cannot use your private key to decrypt information sent to a different user's public key. That's how blockchain cryptography ensures that information can only be accessed by the intended user.

From time to time, you'll come across concerns about the security of blockchain assets in discussions online. Cryptocurrency and any other blockchain assets in your portfolio will only ever be as safe as you make them. In the same way, money in your bank is safe unless you give someone your password. One notable difference is that if your bank account is ever compromised, you might have legal solutions. For example, your bank insures money in your accounts, so if you lose money from the bank's misgivings, they'll find a way to sort things out.

Even if your account was hacked, or someone stole your money by exploiting a weakness on your side, you might still have legal solutions to recover your money. In the cryptocurrency world, you don't have these benefits. Remember that this is a market that thrives on autonomy, and there's no government legislation or regulation so far that protects you in case of loss. Therefore, your crypto wallet is your first and best line of defense.

There are two ways to approach the use of crypto wallets, though these are only guidelines and are not cast in stone. If you are a frequent trader and mostly trade in small amounts, it makes sense to leave your cryptocurrency stored on the exchange. On the other hand, if you hold large amounts of cryptocurrency, you are better off withdrawing most of it to a crypto wallet, giving you more control over your account balances and your private keys.

Hot Crypto Wallets

There are different types of crypto wallets on the market today. However, they all fall under two distinct categories: hot wallets and cold wallets. Hot wallets are software-based online storage facilities, while cold wallets are physical storage.

From our brief description above, the biggest distinction between hot and cold wallets is internet access. Hot wallets are always online, while cold wallets are offline—except when they're being accessed by their owner. There are unique benefits and risks to each alternative. For example, online storage makes your work easier. You can access the content of your wallet from anywhere in the world at any time. On the other hand, this convenience might also be the biggest flaw in this system. Online wallets are always prime targets for hackers. Thus, you have to go the extra mile to protect your hot wallet. Here are some examples:

Web-based Wallets

These are crypto wallets that exist online, and you can only access them through the assigned apps or web browser. In this case, you entrust the security of your private keys to the custodians behind the wallet service.

For someone who is new to blockchain assets, this might seem like a brilliant idea, since you leave the security concerns to custodians, hoping that they have the technical capacity to protect your digital assets. Unfortunately, trusting someone to protect your keys comes with unique challenges.

From our understanding of the function of crypto wallets, they don't really hold your assets, but the keys to them. Since your crypto assets are always live on the blockchain, it's quite possible that the custodian that stores your keys might actually own your coins. What they choose to do with that power is up to them.

Even with different encryption protocols in place, your keys are still stored on a server that you have no control over. By using such a storage platform, you put so much faith in the custodian to hash your keys and take all necessary measures to ensure your keys are always protected from hackers.

The problem here is that custodians are businesses, and every business has its own bottom line and objectives that you might not be privy to. There's always a risk that the custodian could maintain copies of user private keys, possibly to exploit their accounts in the future.

Besides, the fact that your hashed private keys are stored on a central server makes them a honeypot for criminals, considering the number of keys held on the server, and the cumulative value of the accounts they unlock. Therefore, as much as you trust the custodian to protect your digital assets, you will always be vulnerable to their vulnerabilities.

Another problem that might arise is from your end. Your custodian might do all they can to protect user accounts, but their efforts become futile if you create a weak account password.

Desktop Wallets

These are computer programs you can install on your laptop or PC to manage and store your private keys. Desktop wallets offer the same storage and management services as other types of wallets. However, they generally have more features than their counterparts. There are many cross-platform wallets, so whether you are running Linux, Windows, or Mac, you should be covered.

Given the multiplicity of functions in different desktop wallets, it might be difficult to nail down the right wallet to use. Notably, all cryptocurrencies have a core wallet you can download as a desktop wallet. Such wallets are feature-ladden, and you can even run the full node versions.

A full node wallet basically means downloading the entire blockchain on your device. This might only make sense if you have a lot of space to spare on your computer. For example, the Bitcoin full node takes more than 300 GB. On the other hand, Ethereum has proven to be quite a versatile blockchain, and a full node requires more than 700 GB considering the variety of functions it serves.

Other than their space demands, it takes longer to sync the full node, especially if your device has been offline for a while. Even if you have the luxury of storage space, a full node isn't really necessary, unless you intend to participate in validating blocks. The beauty of full nodes, however, is that once installed on your computer, they run just like every other program, so you don't need any special skills to use your wallet. In fact, as long as you can trade on a crypto exchange, you have what it takes to manage a desktop wallet.

Compared to mobile wallets, desktop wallets are more secure. However, they still don't offer the level of security you can get from a hardware wallet, simply because as long as you are connected to the internet, there's always a chance that you might be a victim of a malicious exploit.

Updating the blockchain on a full node takes time and will mostly depend on your internet speed. It can take anywhere from a few days to weeks to complete a sync. However, if your connection is interrupted before you complete the updates, you'll have to start afresh. That sounds like too much work for beginners or regular crypto users. Full nodes would be more practical for expert crypto users, though, as they offer the freedom to validate and verify transactions.

If you don't need the full functionalities of full node wallets, you can install lite wallets, also known as simple payment verification (SPV) wallets. These wallets simply connect users to the cryptocurrency network without having to download the entire blockchain. You can also verify payments using lite wallets.

Mobile Wallets

These are hot wallets that are available as mobile apps that you can install on your phone or tablet. The growth of cryptocurrency coincides with the rapid growth of mobile use globally. Today, most successful businesses have mobile versions of their web-based platforms. Therefore, even though many people still find cryptocurrencies relatively intimidating, mobile apps create a relatable and easier way in. Mobile wallets are mostly lite wallets, so you don't have to worry about mobile computing resources.

Ultimately, hot wallets offer convenience and easy access to your crypto assets. However, these are also their major points of weakness. If you own lots of cryptocurrencies, you definitely don't want to keep them all in hot wallets. Either way, you'll still need to use hot wallets from time to time, so it's more sensible to research and find a platform with robust encryption protocols.

Cold Crypto Wallets

Cold wallets are completely offline. This mode makes them more secure than hot wallets, which are usually prime targets for hackers. However, being offline also makes cold wallets quite an inconvenience. Paper wallets and hardware wallets are two examples of cold wallets you can consider to protect your crypto assets. Let's discuss them briefly below:

Paper Wallets

This is simply a piece of paper with your private and public keys printed or written down on it. Despite the physical risks of losing a piece of paper, this simple note is much safer than a hot wallet. The only possible risks you might incur are the normal ones, like losing the sheet of paper, shredding it to pieces, water damage, fire, and so on. Your crypto assets might be unrecoverable if you lose the paper wallet, so it's always safer to create copies for added security.

Hardware Wallet

This is an external storage device like a Bluetooth device or USB where you can store your crypto keys. To protect your assets from criminal elements, you must physically push a button on the hardware wallet to sign transactions. Therefore, unless someone has physical access to your hardware wallet, they can't do anything to your crypto assets.

It's always safer to store crypto assets you don't need to access immediately in a cold storage wallet. While cold wallets give you that peace of mind, you must also understand that you assume full responsibility for the security of your wallets and assets.

Experts generally advise against keeping your private and public keys together. This way, even if someone comes across one of them, they'll still have the challenge of trying to figure out their compatible match. For offline storage devices, you can get a safe deposit box or any other security mechanism for added protection.

The choice between hot or cold storage wallets depends on your immediate needs. Each of these wallets has unique benefits and potential challenges you might encounter in use, so always weigh your options against your needs and compare different varieties available on the market for each category.

Custodial vs. Non-Custodial Wallets

Apart from the distinction between cold and hot wallets, we can also classify wallets as custodial or non-custodial. This classification is based on token control. For different reasons, many people prefer the crypto wallets issued by cryptocurrency exchanges. Most of these wallets are custodial.

Custodial wallets are typically easy to use. They are great for convenience, making them ideal for day traders and beginner traders. What sets custodial wallets apart from the types of wallets we discussed earlier is that, in this case, you don't have full control over your tokens. The crypto exchange you use keeps your private keys.

We briefly discussed the role of private keys earlier, their significance in protecting your crypto portfolio, and why you should keep them safe all the time. With this in mind, custodial wallets naturally demand that you put your trust in the exchange or service provider to have strict measures in place to secure your tokens.

To this end, the service providers behind custodial wallets have measures in place to protect your wallets from unauthorized access. For example, you'll receive email notifications confirming transactions. Other security measures include biometric authentication (fingerprint verification or facial recognition) and two-factor authentication. You cannot make a transaction until you set up these security checks on most exchanges.

Apart from these user-determined security measures, the custodial wallet service providers take additional measures to protect your tokens. For example, the companies generally transfer a fraction of your funds to their cold storage wallets where they are safe from potential online threats. Some providers even have insurance policies to protect the customer funds in their custody.

Implementing all the security features, plus insurance, available in custodial wallets can be too expensive for an individual user. This is why it might be advisable to use custodial wallets when you are just getting started with crypto trading.

If you wish to retain full control of your tokens, non-custodial wallets might be good for you. When setting up your wallet, you must note down a list of 12 random words generated automatically. These words become your recovery phrase, also known as a mnemonic or seed phrase. It's through this phrase that your private and public keys will be generated. Therefore, in case you are unable to access your device, this phrase acts as your recovery or backup tool.

Note that as long as someone has access to your recovery phrase, they might be able to get full access and control of the contents of your crypto wallet. Thus, if you lose your recovery phrase, your funds might as well be lost. For security reasons, keep your recovery phrase secure. Common methods people use that are not advisable include keeping a photo of the phrase on their phone, printing it out, or keeping a digital copy of it.

From our discussion above, it's clear that hardware wallets are basically non-custodial wallets, seeing that the device already holds the private keys. You can, however, compare different software-based non-custodial wallets available on the market and choose one that suits your needs. Remember that the most important thing is to have full control of your tokens.

Ultimately, whoever holds your private keys also owns your tokens. This is one of the reasons why many people tend to shy away from custodial wallets. You put a lot of trust in the service provider, hoping that they will act diligently with your investments. Perhaps the advantage you have is that you might have some sort of reprieve in the event of a breach. For example, if your service provider has insurance protection, you could get some or all of your crypto assets back, among other recovery alternatives they might have in place. With non-custodial wallets, you are on your own. You have no reprieve if you lose the recovery phrase.

Considering the distinct features of these wallets, choosing the best of the two comes down to your personal preferences and investment needs. Custodial wallets are a good option if you have a history of losing devices from time to time, or if you struggle with password management. In this case, take advantage of the backup options and other security methods put in place by exchange service providers.

Additionally, custodial wallets generally have lower transaction fees, while some are free, making them perfect for beginners with little or no crypto trading experience. If none of this works for you, non-custodial wallets might be the way to go.

Multi-Signature Wallets

Multi-signature wallets, also known as multi-sig wallets, provide added security by requiring two or more private key signatures to authorize transactions. Using more than one key signature can protect you from losing your wallet if you ever lose one key. For example, if you have three keys and lose one, you can still sign transactions with the other two.

The need for multiple signatures also makes these wallets ideal for fraud prevention, especially with institutional wallets like exchanges, hedge fund accounts, and corporate wallets. In such cases, the wallet is set up to require a certain key majority to authorize transactions. Therefore, it becomes impossible for one person to authorize transactions and steal from the institution. Unilateral authorization has always been a challenge for many organizations, where individuals pilfer company resources by exploiting their administrative rights to the accounts. Multi-sig wallets eliminate this problem.

Which is the best wallet for you?

The short answer is—there's no right or wrong option.

All the wallets we've discussed above have significant benefits and potential drawbacks you should be aware of. However, take note that there are multi-sig wallet versions for all the types of wallets we've discussed in this section. So, apart from considering the pros and cons, it would be wise to use multi-sig versions of whichever wallet you choose, just so you don't get locked out when you lose one key.

Ultimately, the best wallet comes down to your needs. Whether you seek convenience, compatibility (especially in NFT markets), or long-term storage, there are lots of options to consider. That being said, here are some important factors that can help you compare the features of competing wallets:

- how long the wallet has been on the market

- backup options

- user-friendliness

- native coins supported

- security features

- affordability

- integration with decentralized apps or decentralized exchanges (if you need it)

- compatibility with different computing platforms

- user reviews

As a rule of thumb, never store all your crypto assets in a single wallet. Ideally, for most people, the choice comes down to security and convenience. With this in mind, an ideal solution would be a careful mix of hot and cold wallets with multi-sig variation where necessary.

Chapter 7: Air Drops

Companies use different methods to gauge the market response before they release a new product. Sales promotions, discounts, and offers are common methods that have been widely successful over the years. Brands use the responses to refine the final product, create engagement, and many other benefits to give the product the perfect launch. Crypto airdrops espouse the same concept.

In the simplest terms, crypto airdrops are a marketing ploy to drum up support for a crypto project. Airdrops are generally part of an elaborate marketing initiative aimed at encouraging users to engage with a project. Project developers send free tokens to community members hoping for some kind of engagement, even if that engagement is limited to figuring out how to cash out the tokens into a currency they prefer.

While the end-game in many crypto projects might be getting users to spend money at some point, airdrops are primarily used to create awareness. Some of the common requests from project owners in exchange for free tokens in the new project include requesting users to follow their project account pages on social media, conduct crypto transactions using their wallets or platforms, retweet or share their posts and hashtags, or join their mailing list for frequent updates on the project. There are also occasional instances where project owners release airdrops without asking for something in return.

From an investor's point of view, crypto airdrops can be an excellent opportunity to increase the diversity in your portfolio without necessarily spending your money. If you are active in crypto communities, there's a good chance you might come across a few airdrops, which might turn out to be incredible investments in the future. On top of that, airdrops might also give you front-row access to an exciting new project without spending your money.

While airdrops seem like amazing investment opportunities, particularly for beginners who might not have a lot of money to commit, you must also be aware that airdrops might prove worthless. Just like we have seen in promotional strategies before, not all products make the cut. Some products are usually introduced to test the market and once the promotional period is over, we'll never hear about them again. The same applies to airdrops.

As much as the prospect of the airdrop might be exciting, it's prudent to research and learn more about the project before you spend so much time and possibly money. Some airdrop projects get devalued even before you get the chance to sell them, killing any chance of profit-making you might have had. In most such cases, the project simply couldn't live up to its expectations. You might even think of the prospectus as a house of cards.

Since you didn't pay anything for the tokens, the failure of such a project might not be much of a bother. However, some projects are laced with sinister objectives, so even without losing money on the project, you could still suffer great losses. There's always a risk of sharing privileged information with a fraudulent entity. In the age of data mining and other ills around the fraudulent acquisition of user data, you might never truly know what the entities behind the airdrop project intend to do with your data. Thus, one should always exercise extreme caution when engaging in airdrop projects.

Airdrop Utility

Now that you understand the promotional role of airdrops, you can go further and probe the inherent value of the airdrop. What do you get out of it? Better yet, what do the project founders get out of it? This will help you evaluate the utility value of the airdrop, and more importantly, if it's worth your time.

To determine whether the project will be valuable to you or not, you must first understand how airdrops work. Every airdrop is unique to the project it's meant to promote. However, they mostly follow the same structure. An upcoming airdrop could be promoted on airdrop-relevant websites, social media, or the project's website, including information on how to sign up for the airdrop.

While the idea of an airdrop might be exciting for a lot of users, not everyone is eligible. The project owners usually include specific requirements that participants must meet or actions they must complete to participate in the airdrop. For example, you might be required to own a specific cryptocurrency, or join the project's group, or follow their page on social media.

The airdrop will take place once you complete the required steps. The project owners will then distribute the cryptocurrency to the wallets of participants who meet their requirements. In some instances, project owners use smart contracts to complete the airdrop. After the transfer, you should see the airdropped cryptocurrency in your account instantly. Similarly, the total number of the cryptocurrency in circulation will instantly increase now that more users have the cryptocurrency in their digital wallets.

So, why are airdrops necessary?

Economic Value

Well, as a promotional strategy, airdrops are all about numbers. Having the coins in circulation is a simple way of creating economic value for them. Naturally, those who receive the cryptocurrency in their wallets will initiate conversations about them. You'll probably want to know how to convert the coins into a cryptocurrency you use frequently, or fiat currency.

Other than creating exponential economic activity around the cryptocurrency, airdrops also help to influence the value of the new currency. The coin's value can only increase if people are using it. For example, if a gaming company issues airdrops, they'll probably want gamers to use the currency for in-game assets. As more people use the currency within the game, its value increases. This is common in play-to-earn games.

Value is also a function of the number of people using or investing in the new currency. By encouraging more people to use it, the volume of transactions increases, and, similarly, the number of people who own the currency increases. Ultimately, this drives up the coin's value in the market.

We can also highlight the psychological aspect of airdrops. Borrowing from the success of Bitcoin, it's in your best interest to make sure that the currency you are invested in performs well in the market. Therefore, if all it takes is to talk about it and create awareness among other users, you'll do all you can to broaden the audience, especially if the coin gets listed on an exchange. More conversations around the coin increase the likelihood of price appreciation.

User Appreciation

Unlike in the traditional investment market, most investors in the crypto ecosystem are hardly concerned about the long-term gains of their investment or its sustainability.

Their interest is mostly in their return on investment (ROI). This might also explain why many crypto investors keep jumping from one project to the next.

Such investors don't drive any value in the market, especially those who invest large sums of money. They are always chasing quick wins and never stay on a project long enough to realize its potential. The problem with having such investors in a project is that they ultimately damage the project. It's all good when they pump in their money, but it won't last long as they'll soon be on their way in their pursuit of the next big thing.

To deal with this nuisance, crypto projects started issuing airdrops as a reward mechanism to loyal investors who stay with them for a while. By keeping your money in the project, you continually use the platform, and create and sustain value in it, earning rights to receive free coins in an airdrop.

Sensitization

For a long time, many new blockchain projects relied on crowdfunding. ICOs were quite popular. However, ICOs soon became a haven for criminals. Fraudsters would copy white papers from successful projects, carefully edit them to portray a new project, and then obtain money from unsuspecting investors.

After one too many incidents, investors started avoiding ICOs. Countries like China, for example, have imposed a blanket ban on ICOs. In the U.S., ICOs targeting local investors are now under intense scrutiny from the SEC to ensure that all their activities are above board. However, even with these institutional interventions, the reputation of ICOs was beyond salvation.

To get through this, legitimate founders needed a better approach to spur attention to a new project. What better way to create confidence in a project than by issuing free coins to potential investors? It works well for them too, because they get free marketing from the airdrop recipients. By issuing a small fraction of their tokens to the public, they are assured of organic growth and expansion. For a market whose value is mostly driven by speculation, there's nothing better than creating a community around it, especially one that grows naturally.

The Need for Decentralization

Centralization is often a risk in the early days of a blockchain project. Investors generally research the project before pumping their money into it. For the project owners, receiving the money is a good thing. They can invest it in line with their prospectus. However, this also creates another problem, control.

If you have a few wealthy investors bringing their money to your project, they are mostly getting it at a bargain, as everyone else is. The only problem here is that most of the coins in circulation will be in the hands of a few individuals, creating an element of centralization. This spells trouble for the project in case any of these investors leaves the project or is hacked. One way of solving this problem is by issuing airdrops. Issuing coins to other users evens out the distribution in an attempt to restore the true sense of decentralization in the project.

Now that you understand the important role of airdrops in a crypto project, how do you qualify for one?

Considering the various reasons why project owners would issue airdrops, it's not easy to determine whether you qualify for one or not. Eligibility is mostly based on the unique requirements of the project and whether it suits your investment objectives. Therefore, you might come across an airdrop that seems exciting and you are eligible, but if it doesn't meet your investment goals, it wouldn't make sense to participate in it.

You can monitor social media updates for news on upcoming airdrops, usually with the hashtag #airdrop. You can also research crypto communities online to learn about websites dedicated to airdrops. If you come across these, you can simply sign up to receive updates the same way you sign up for promotional information from online stores and other websites you frequent.

More often, information on airdrops and other exciting blockchain projects is freely available in blockchain communities. Thus, being an active participant in such avenues can also help you learn more about upcoming airdrops.

Even with this information, the basic requirement to receive airdrops is to have an active cryptocurrency wallet. You might still use an address issued to you by an exchange, but this might not always be suitable for airdrops. There are quite a number of secure crypto wallet providers out there, so you can research and choose one that meets your financial and investment needs.

Pros and Cons

Like every financial investment, always weigh the pros and cons before investing your time and resources into airdrops. This gives you a clearer perspective, not just on the airdrop but also on the potential project you are buying into. Let's explore some of the benefits in-depth below.

- **Diversified Portfolio**

Airdrops can be an awesome opportunity to build a stronger portfolio. The fact that you are getting free tokens makes it even better because if the project turns out to be a success, you'll have diversified and grown your portfolio with free digital assets.

- **Early Bird Benefits**

At the same time, airdrops also give you early access to potentially huge projects before everyone else gets in. The concept might not have been around when Bitcoin was being floated in the market in its early days, but imagine how amazing it would have been to buy into a Bitcoin airdrop in 2009 and hold onto your assets for a few more years.

- **The Quest for Knowledge**

Airdrops can also be a great opportunity to learn about new projects and their potential. As a promotional strategy, potential investors will try to find out more about the project behind the airdrop. Remember that, ultimately, airdrops are meant to encourage your investment in the project.

What's the project about? What problems are they trying to solve? What's their value proposition? How do they address security? These are some of the important issues investors must know about a project. Without this information, or if you can only get vague responses, it's highly likely the project might not have any tangible value, and might even be a scam.

As a rule of thumb, always approach an airdrop project with the same prudence you approach bonds, IPOs, and other investments in the traditional financial market. After all, the end goal is to commit your hard-earned money to the project.

Now, let's discuss some potential pitfalls of airdrops.

- **Prohibitive Entry**

As all airdrops are unique to the parent project's needs, there's a chance that you might not be comfortable with some of the eligibility requirements. For example, the obligation to publicly post the project on your social media account might not sit well with everyone.

Your social media account is private property, and you reserve the right to use it as you please. Maybe you are a private person, or you restrict your social media posts to social activities. Such a requirement can force you out of your comfort zone. Besides, this could also lock you out of the project if you don't have a social media account.

Some airdrops require ownership of specific coins to create some economic activity in the project. For various reasons, you might not fancy the coins in question, or you simply might not have them, missing out on the opportunity. More often, such projects also require participants to use specific digital wallets, which you might like.

- **Tax Liability**

Your free tokens might not be as free as you think they are. The IRS, for example, considers income from airdrops as taxable income. Failure to account for this while filing your tax returns could result in some serious problems with the IRS.

- **Potential for Fraud**

Some people say ICOs crawled so airdrops could walk. While airdrops have helped many project owners create interest in their projects and ultimately create value, criminal elements in the blockchain ecosystem have also realized their potential and have massively exploited airdrops. At the moment, the blockchain ecosystem is awash with news of airdrop phishing scams. These are elaborate ploys to trick you into connecting your digital wallet to a fake project, where the criminals eventually wipe your wallets clean.

- **Buying Into Nothing**

A potential challenge investors experience with airdrops is the loss of value. As a speculative investment, users hope that they can gain from the value appreciation when they sell the coins. However, there's a possibility of the coin's price falling before you can sell it.

Unfortunately, some airdrops are simply worthless. Even though you might get free coins, it's quite disheartening when you realize you wasted your time and effort researching a project that has no potential for growth or tangible value.

- **The Freeloader Problem**

Since airdrops are a sure guarantee of free coins, many project owners run the risk of having lots of freeloaders on their platform. These are users who only drum up the numbers but don't add any value to the project. For example, an airdrop can help you grow the social media channels, but not all the numbers on the channel translate to reliable investors. You could join a Telegram channel with more than 100,000 users, yet barely half of that number are active investors.

People love freebies. For this reason, airdrop hunters will always prowl the internet looking for the next opportunity to score some free tokens. As soon as they achieve their target, they quit the social media groups and move on to the next target.

There's also the ethical issue where some project owners buy social media followers to create the illusion of a project with massive public buy-in. This can dupe unsuspecting investors into investing in the project, only for it to flop as soon as it takes off because, in the real sense, there wasn't any value in the project from the beginning.

Considering the risks above, airdrops might be an exciting way into new blockchain projects, but not necessarily for everyone. Most people who benefit from airdrops are crypto enthusiasts, given their in-depth knowledge of the market, especially those who actively manage their crypto portfolios. However, this shouldn't deter you either, since all the enthusiasts and experts on blockchain matters were beginners at some point.

Types of Airdrops

There are five main types of airdrops that project owners use to entice potential investors into their projects. The main difference between these airdrops is in the eligibility criteria, as shown below:

1. Standard Airdrop

Standard airdrops are open to anyone willing to participate. The project owners distribute small amounts of the token to your digital wallet in exchange for some action. For example, you might be asked to join a mailing list. The project owners could also request to complete a Know Your Customer (KYC) process before receiving the airdrop. In such cases, they'll request your wallet and email address.

2. Bounty Airdrop

Bounty airdrops are often used to reward users who prop up the project's promotion strategy. They mostly request users to promote the project's content on social media. For example, you might be asked to follow the brand account, share or retweet their posts, and so on. Some project owners make the bounty experience more alluring by offering more airdrops for referrals.

3. Exclusive Airdrop

Unlike the first two airdrops, this lot comes with no strings attached. The no-obligation airdrops are distributed to loyal users, participants, contributors, or followers of a crypto project. They are offered by airdrop aggregators and websites who prioritize users who consistently engage on their platforms.

4. Holder Airdrop

Holder airdrops are reserved for users who already own some coins or tokens in a project. For example, if you are an avid user of the Ethereum blockchain, you might receive free tokens for a new project built on the Ethereum blockchain.

The project owners take a snapshot of everyone's holdings in their project at a specified time, after which users are invited to claim their airdrops according to their wallet holdings at the time of the snapshot.

5. Hard Fork Airdrop

Hard fork airdrops are atypical of the other four. A hard fork is the result of a dynamic change in the protocol code of a project such that a completely new token is created. When this happens, you end up with two versions of the blockchain, the old one following the old rules, while the new one ascribes to the new protocols.

A hard fork airdrop could be used after this split, earning users of the original protocol an equal number of the new token in their wallets. Since they've been using the old protocol and it probably has a thriving economy built around it, a hard fork airdrop can similarly help to create an instant economic activity for the new tokens.

Airdrop Scams

Despite their appeal, airdrops haven't always been a safe bet, especially for beginner investors who are still trying to figure their way around the market. Like their predecessors, the ICOs, criminal elements have found their way into the airdrop ecosystem, and you have to be careful when assessing potential investments.

Since airdrops basically offer free money, they can be used as pump and dump schemes. This is a situation where project founders issue tokens through airdrops to create hype around the project. While there's nothing wrong with this, their intention is usually to have the token listed on an exchange. Listing a token on an exchange usually instills confidence in some investors, because they believe the project must have met stringent requirements to be listed. Unfortunately, this isn't always the case.

The crypto market is unlike the traditional financial market, where companies must pass through a series of checks, including the IRS and the SEC, before they list on an exchange. Without stringent regulations, criminal project creators only need to create enough hype to get their project on an exchange. As soon as it starts trading, they sell a large number of the tokens, crashing the price in the process, and you end up holding worthless tokens.

Another potential scam is a dusting attack. These attacks go against the anonymity principle of blockchain solutions. While all activities on the blockchain are visible to the public (hence operational transparency), user account details are always anonymized. This is what dusting attacks go after.

In such an attack, the criminals will send tokens to user wallets to track their activities and, through different analytical processes, try to decode the company or individual behind the wallet.

You also have phishing scams where you are redirected to a scam website to redeem your tokens. By keying in your information, the fraudsters have everything they need from you. Others use fake keys and fake airdrops to collect your private keys and steal your crypto assets.

If you come across an exciting airdrop, learn more about the project. Find out who owns it, their leadership structure, the prospectus, and anything else that can help you understand what the project is about. Join online communities and discussions about that project so you can gauge what other investors think or feel about it before you rush to claim the airdrop. These brief moments of insight could save you a fortune.

Remember that in the blockchain ecosystem, you are always your first and best line of defense. Never disclose your private keys to anyone. On the same note, research well before connecting your wallet to any third party. If you are ever in doubt, ask a question in online crypto forums so you don't put your investments at risk. Ultimately, as long as you own some cryptocurrency in a digital wallet, you can think of yourself as a personal bank. If you lose your private keys or if your wallet gets hacked, it's over for you.

For security reasons, you can always set up a new identity for airdrops. Create a new email and wallet address for this. This becomes your sandbox account for airdrops and anything else you might not be completely certain about.

Finally, despite all the potential challenges you might encounter, airdrops are still a good opportunity to get into promising crypto projects as early investors and make a fortune if the project turns out to be a success.

Chapter 8: Future of Cryptocurrency

From a financial or economic point of view, cryptocurrency is already considered a futuristic concept in many ways. It is a revolutionary idea that has changed the way we perceive money, business, finance, and technology. For many people, cryptography has only ever been the domain of encryption protocols. Since the advent of cryptocurrency and subsequent developments in the blockchain space, we have realized several approaches under which cryptography can be implemented. Thus, the consensus is that the next phase in the evolution of cryptocurrency and the greater blockchain ecosystem is widespread integration into the modern economy.

Naturally, institutional finance is bound to claim its role in the next phase of cryptocurrency. To achieve this, we must also implement regulatory protocols to plug some of the gaping holes in blockchain protocols. Institutional money has thrived behind the backing of strict controls and regulations. The way forward is to figure out how to introduce these aspects into the blockchain ecosystem, which was natively created for decentralized control and trustless operations.

Things are looking up for cryptocurrencies as more merchants start accepting them in their businesses. For widespread acceptance to occur, the uptake must continue at a steady pace. This can only be achieved when both merchants and customers realize and appreciate the inherent value of cryptocurrencies. To achieve this, cryptocurrencies must be easy enough for the average customer with no tech experience to use, while simultaneously being complex enough to guarantee their security.

Another issue that might come up is how to maintain the anonymity guaranteed by blockchain solutions while at the same time warding off criminal elements from exploiting these features for their gain. It's fair to foresee a future where cryptocurrency attributes will evolve to match the need for regulation, as is the case with fiat currencies.

Debate on the future of cryptocurrency will primarily revolve around the two major players in the market—Bitcoin, and Ethereum. Bitcoin's primary contribution to these discussions will be its role as an alternative currency. Lessons will be drawn from the example of El Salvador, the first country to recognize Bitcoin as legal tender. The historical volatility of Bitcoin is another area that will gain more attention, particularly on how to circumvent it and stabilize Bitcoin. It is only until some form of stability is achieved that Bitcoin can truly penetrate the financial systems and be integrated into global economics.

On the other hand, growth in the Ethereum blockchain will continue on the development front, with decentralized applications, finance, and other blockchain projects that leverage the power of smart contracts taking center stage.

As much as cryptocurrency has been a game-changer in the financial sector, there are glaring challenges that will have to be addressed. For example, there's the issue of security. A crashed computer is all it takes to wipe out your digital fortune, assuming that you are unable to recover or restore the computer to its working state. Hackers are on the prowl for vulnerable virtual vaults. However, these are challenges that could be easily addressed with evolving technological solutions.

For investment purposes, cryptocurrencies are an opportunity you should strongly look into. Just like every other speculative investment, understand the risks involved before getting excited by the prospect of great returns. Unlike most traditional investments, it's so easy to lose all your money in cryptocurrencies. These are largely speculative investments, and for that reason, the potential for huge price swings increases your risk of total loss.

Blockchain and the Industrial Sector

Cryptocurrency thrives because of the unique features of blockchain technology. It's imperative, therefore, that we look at how the evolution of blockchain technology will affect the industrial sector. Coming off the impressive impact of Bitcoin and the Ethereum blockchain on society, the blockchain ecosystem can be aptly described as disruptive. Global enterprises have been pushed to rethink their business models to support a seamless integration of blockchain products and the traditional financial system. Customers want this integration, so it's only fair that businesses listen to their needs and figure out how to create a win-win situation for both parties.

As far as business processes are concerned, blockchain trials in different sectors have yielded promising results. Let's have a look at some of the key sectors of our economy where blockchain technology will continue to have a significant impact in the future:

Cybersecurity

Security will always be a concern for the global economy. This concern dates back to the formative years of the internet and has persisted to date. The problem with security is that criminals have access to the same technologies that we use to try and combat crime online. Therefore, as our technologies evolve, so do their innovative approaches to committing crimes online. For that reason, cyberattacks will always be a threat to our digital existence.

So far, the immutability of blockchain technology has been touted as a brilliant way to combat crime. This comes at a time when the importance of data is taking center stage. Data is the new gold. It's also quite exciting because we live in a time when almost every device you use to interact with the internet collects some crucial data about you. From smartphone apps to websites, there's an insatiable demand for user data, and this demand will persist into the future, especially with more Internet of Things (IoT) devices going mainstream. By design, blockchain technology can prevent data manipulation, especially from unauthorized access.

The decentralization concept will also gain a lot of interest in various industries, particularly in projects or solutions where security is of utmost importance. Decentralized security is a brilliant idea in that it eliminates centralized flaws, thereby strengthening security solutions where applicable. The fact that data on the blockchain cannot be tampered with means it's easy to identify the origins of malicious attacks and take corrective or preventive actions immediately.

Banking Sector

Any future advancement in cryptocurrency or blockchain technology is bound to have a ripple effect on the banking sector. For cryptocurrencies whose primary role is operating as alternatives to fiat currency, the banking sector will always be a prime target for disruption. So far, cryptocurrencies have challenged several functions within the banking sector, making people realize the inefficiencies therein and that cryptocurrencies offer exciting solutions.

The disruptive impact of cryptocurrencies on the banking sector can be felt in areas like cost of transactions, ease of conducting business, speed of completing transactions, cheaper cross-border transactions, and so on. With the fact that cryptocurrencies tackle the problem and cost of intermediaries head-on, we can only look to the future with excitement.

It's no secret that banks understand the potential of cryptocurrency and are already looking into ways of getting in on the action. Embracing cryptocurrency will also allow banks access to a new market, the large population of the unbanked or underbanked. For different reasons, millions, if not billions, of users have for a long time been locked out of the institutionalized banking system. By embracing blockchain technology, banks will have to come up with unique products that cater to the needs of this market. Even more interesting will be how to implement blockchain solutions into the banking sector, given the kind of regulations necessary and the fact that blockchain technology thrives without centralized regulation.

Governance

The trustless nature of blockchain technology can be implemented in different aspects of governance. So far, voter fraud is one vice that can be avoided through blockchain technology. Traditional voting has come a long way, with different methods being used all over the world. Today, voting is mostly conducted by queuing to cast votes for candidates or mailing in votes. While each of these methods works and promotes the idea of secret balloting, they have always had unique challenges.

One of the biggest problems with the voting system is its reliance on a central organization to oversee the entire process, from creating the voter register to counting and announcing the votes. Too often, these functions are not void of bias, which is the first point of flaw. Other than the institutionalized bias, there's always the prospect of hacking because of the central voter database.

Each of the issues raised above could be mitigated by blockchain technology. Blockchain voting solutions can even encourage a wider voter turnout because of the assurance of anonymity. In many cases, people generally don't turn up to vote for fear of intimidation, particularly under dictatorial regimes. Blockchain solutions could help overcome such challenges and restore confidence in democratic processes.

Voting is, perhaps, a great example of how blockchain technology can influence changes in the future, but we cannot limit ourselves to it. Many governance functions are often shrouded in impunity, bias, and fraud, to mention a few ills. Tendering processes, for example, could be streamlined through blockchain technology. More often, huge tenders are awarded under scandalous circumstances, denying worthy candidates great opportunities.

We might also see more uptake of blockchain technology in managing registries, not just for digital assets but for all other asset registries in the future. In particular, this might come in handy when registering real estate, cars, or any other instance where notary services might be required. The point of this implementation is to ease not just the registration process but also verification and authentication. Governments might actually find it easier to collect taxes and implement automatic controls to make the tax collection and reporting process easier, thereby reducing fraud.

Ultimately, any form of governance that requires security and transparency could benefit from integrating blockchain technology into its processes. This is an exciting time to consider blockchain technology, given the general pursuit of automation across different sectors. The security and immutability features of blockchain technology will be an added advantage wherever the need for automation is imminent.

Medicine and Healthcare

The healthcare sector has always struggled with data storage. Anyone can view your medical records as long as they can access the central database. On top of that, many hospitals don't have modern data storage methods, so the data is stored manually. In such cases, retrieving information can be an unnecessarily laborious experience. You might not realize it, but the longer it takes to retrieve data, the more chances there are for loss, theft, or breach, wherein your information could be altered for any number of reasons.

Medical records should always be accurate. Inaccuracies could easily result in fatalities because this information is often useful for prescriptions. This is why the immutability of blockchain technology could be a timely asset for the healthcare sector in the future. Personal medical records should always be a private affair, and that can be achieved with the anonymity provided by blockchain technology.

Away from data security, another scourge in the healthcare sector is counterfeiting. The market is flooded with counterfeit medicines, denying patients access to quality drugs, while at the same time denying the legitimate producers their deserved income. One of the challenges of counterfeit medicines is that it's not always easy to distinguish them from authentic medicine. Blockchain solutions can streamline supply chain management and make it easier to track medicines from the pharmacy all the way back to their origins.

Supply Chain Management

Blockchain transparency and immutability can be a great asset in enhancing efficiency in supply chain operations. With these features, it's easier to track all the steps and procedures throughout the supply network. You can record important details on the blockchain like certification, quality, location, date, and timestamps, giving you a better insight into supply chain operations.

Since all this information is available on the blockchain for all relevant parties for reference purposes, it becomes easier to prevent counterfeits, reduce losses from spoilage, theft, and other challenges that affect the overall business process. For outsourcing businesses, these changes can help to improve compliance, especially in instances where products are sourced from different countries.

For example, retailers can track agricultural products back to the farmer. In case some of the produce goes bad or doesn't meet the minimum quality standards, it's easier to address the issue with the individual farmer, instead of taking all their farm produce off the shelves, affecting even those farmers who delivered good quality produce. Blockchain technology can also be used to implement verification protocols at different levels, helping businesses address and avoid illegal operations by rogue employees.

Insurance

Forgeries and fraudulent claims are some of the common problems that affect the insurance business. These, together with rising costs of doing business, generally result in massive losses for insurers.

At the moment, most blockchain integrations focus on cost reduction. Insurance companies can achieve significant cost savings through Blockchain solutions in administration, claims, underwriting, product development, and management. Most of these benefits can be realized by automating processes and implementing additional verification procedures. Payments between customers, insurers, and reinsurers can be automated, reducing the average cost of administration and time involved in completing contractual commitments.

Blockchain technology can also be used to enhance evidence collection methods for underwriters. Through digital evidence collection, it's easier to incorporate records into the underwriting process, further enhancing the cost and process of product development and service delivery.

Transport and Logistics

The transport and logistics industry is one sector where inefficiencies cost companies a lot of money every year. These can be addressed at different levels, from administration and back office operations to the truckers on the road. One area where blockchain solutions can be useful is in enhancing the traceability of goods from ports to the final customer's intended destination.

Success or failure in the commercial transport and logistics sector generally depends on the company's ability to meet changing customer needs. This usually comes down to efficiency challenges, and rising costs of doing business. Most of these issues can be addressed through strategic blockchain integrations in various business processes.

Blockchain technology can also help in dispute resolution and improve the payment processes. This can reduce the average wait time for companies to get paid. Payment delays eventually add up to the administrative costs, which are already slowed down by the traditional paper transaction approaches.

In a tracking experiment by Maersk and IBM, it became apparent that a container shipping flowers to the port of Rotterdam in the Netherlands from Mombasa, Kenya was handled by at least 30 organizations. From the point of dispatch to its final delivery, more than 200 communication channels were opened to facilitate all logistical requirements for the container. Throughout the communication and handling process, important documents were exchanged, without which the shipment could have been delayed or held back at the dispatching port indefinitely.

This goes to show just how important blockchain technology can be in this industry. All the information needed to process the shipment at any point of contact could be available on the blockchain, making it easier for the relevant authorities to perform their due diligence on the shipment, reducing the risk of delay.

Apart from delivery logistics, blockchain solutions can also be implemented in fleet management, including the performance history of a truck. This creates a dependable database, especially for businesses that rely on used trucks. All information about the performance of a truck is made available on the blockchain, including the repair and maintenance history and schedules.

Indeed, there are companies that are already providing such in-depth information about used cars, but they operate as intermediaries in the vehicle sales business, driving up the costs further. Instead of paying intermediaries for this information, you should be able to access it on the blockchain to verify the vehicle's roadworthiness and whether it suits your business needs.

Conclusion

Cryptocurrency has come a long way, yet in many ways, it is still considered, in some cases, an emerging technology. This is further compounded by the volatility and unpredictability witnessed in the market recently. There are still several concerns around the development of cryptocurrencies, and in particular, advancing the technology into mainstream industries and gaining widespread acceptance and adoption. Yet, one thing that we can be certain about is that cryptocurrencies are here to stay, and their revolutionary impact on global economics will help to speed up the next crucial phase in the development of finance and the internet.

We can think of cryptocurrency as a radical, or even a political feature because of the manner in which they have challenged our conventional thoughts and actions around finance, governance, and authority. Our society operates under the notion that freedoms and rights can only be obtained from and maintained by the government or any other central authority upon which such mandates are conferred. Through blockchain technology, cryptocurrencies open our eyes to the possibility of governance by immutable code. In financial matters, this takes away the leverage that banks, brokers, and other institutions have always held over their customers.

Considering the sheer weight of the revolutionary changes being proposed through different cryptocurrency projects, it's easy to see why privacy and regulation concerns are of utmost importance when dealing with cryptocurrency.

We have outlined an in-depth discussion on cryptocurrency, from foundational concepts to forecasting the future, in the hope that you will get the best introduction to this revolutionary aspect of finance. Despite some of the challenges that have befallen cryptocurrencies since they went mainstream, the hype phase is gone, and we are currently in the phase where blockchain technology is helping advance amazing solutions in society. By all means, this is the best time to learn not just about cryptocurrency, but also about the utility value that lies therein.

Earlier on, most people invested in cryptocurrency hoping to gain from capital appreciation, assuming that the price of the currency appreciated after they bought it. While that is still the case, there are far more valuable applications of blockchain technology that you can invest in and which can act as a tangible source of passive income. The freedom that comes with passive income is something many investors look forward to, because in the long run, passive income is one of the gateways to financial independence in the future. Therefore, it's safe to say that you are not just investing in cryptocurrency, you are investing in your future.

Everything we have discussed so far will go a long way in helping you find your footing in the world of cryptocurrency and blockchain technology in general. From investing in the next big ICO to participating in some of the DeFi products you can come across, there's so much to look forward to for investment purposes. That being said, we cannot turn a blind eye to the fact that there's always risk imminent in cryptocurrencies. This, unfortunately, is true of all kinds of investments, even those that are considered to be safe. If anything, the imminence of risk raises the potential threshold for returns on an investment. This is a common concept in finance, where high risks are often associated with the potential for high returns.

Other than the common risks inherent in every investment, you must also exercise precaution to protect your investment portfolio from fraud, theft, and loss. We mentioned the importance of this in our definitions of online and offline wallets. While your online wallet makes it easier for you to access your cryptocurrencies, buy and sell them, you must be careful not to fall victim to rampant hacking attempts. On the other hand, storing your cryptocurrencies offline is a feasible solution, but if you lose your physical storage device, you might never be able to recover your assets.

Ultimately, investing in cryptocurrency is a brilliant idea, mostly because of its transformative nature. Blockchain technology has so much potential and, given its immutability, could be a reliable asset in different sectors, including running an election. If you've ever spoken to a real estate agent about the process of purchasing a house, you'll be aware of how tedious it is and all the paperwork involved. Every additional party to the contract drives up the overall cost by some margin, which is reflected in the closing costs. But, with cryptocurrency, the purchase or sale can be as simple as a contract between the buyer and the seller, with all the terms of the contract coded into the smart contract.

The choice you have to make is whether cryptocurrency is a good investment for you or not. Like all other investments, this isn't a decision you should make lightly. Regardless of what happens in the cryptocurrency market, your decision should be guided by personal goals and objectives. For example, what do you expect from your investment portfolio in five or ten years? How much growth do you wish to recognize in that time? How does cryptocurrency fit into this plan? This approach is more wholesome than simply responding with a yes or no to whether cryptocurrency is a good investment or not.

Generally, high-risk investments like cryptocurrency should only constitute a small fraction of your portfolio. This protects your portfolio from the erosive impact of a highly volatile market. Before you invest in cryptocurrency, therefore, make sure you set aside some money for emergencies and invest some in relatively safer instruments like bonds.

Even with a carefully diversified portfolio of cryptocurrencies and other investments, you must never forget to research an opportunity before committing your funds to it. Try and find out the prospects of the cryptocurrency, who is backing it, and more importantly, the kind of conversations going on in the community backing it. This would be a good time to join the Telegram and Discord conversations to learn more about the future prospects and any potential challenges that community members foresee.

Credible or reputable cryptocurrencies usually have the kind of information investors need publicly available. Information on things like the overall market capitalization or the number of transactions processed daily should be easily available online. Monitor these for a few weeks before you can make a decision. If you notice a general trend of growth in the currency's transactions, this might be a sign of its utility value to investors.

As a rule of thumb, never invest in any cryptocurrency project without reading the published white paper. A white paper is like a prospectus, explaining the important details about the crypto project, such as the protocol for distributing tokens, the core functions of the project, and the individuals and brands backing or heading the project.

More importantly, find out whether your purchase entitles you to ownership of the tokens or the company. Buying into a company entitles you to ownership rights, like sharing in the profits. On the other hand, if your ownership is limited to the tokens, then the most you stand to benefit from the project is utilizing the tokens for whichever purpose they were created.

There's so much to look forward to in the future of cryptocurrency. Perhaps, someday, cryptocurrencies might even be floated and traded on the major stock exchanges like Nasdaq, making it easier for more people to appreciate their utility value and trust in the projects since listing usually comes with a lot of disclosures and regulations.

Now that you are ready to trade in cryptocurrencies, handle this investment with the same caution you'd handle every other investment in your financial portfolio. Understand the risks and the fact that there's always a chance you might lose everything. Research well and stay informed on international matters concerning cryptocurrencies and the blockchain ecosystem in general. Since it might not be easy to anticipate price swings as you would in the traditional financial market, being well-informed could go a long way in helping you preempt some drastic changes in the market, which in turn can help limit your exposure to losses.

Finally, opinion will always be split on the viability of cryptocurrencies as viable investment tools. That being said, cryptocurrencies are continuously evolving, and as more people adopt and integrate them into their lives, their tangible value increases. As we saw in chapter four about crypto myths, most opinions people peddle around are heresy and half-truths which you can factually address with some research work. Your perception of risk will go a long way in making informed decisions about investing in cryptocurrency. Remember that cryptocurrency projects aren't always the same, so even though some might be quite popular, always try and understand the risks involved before committing your money. Treat this as an investment opportunity, not a chance to get rich quickly.

Glossary

Altcoin

Altcoin, from the words alternative and coin, is a word used to represent all cryptocurrencies apart from Bitcoin. However, the term has also been used to represent alternative coins to Bitcoin and Ethereum, since most cryptocurrencies in existence are forks of either Bitcoin or Ethereum.

Buy the Dip

A common investment strategy is to buy an asset after the price has fallen. The assumption here is that the asset is available for a bargain at the new price, and you'll make considerable profits when the price starts rising.

Blockchain

A digital transaction ledger that is distributed through computer networks all over the world, which is also the foundation technology on which cryptocurrencies are created and operate. Information written on the blockchain is immutable, which means that it cannot be altered once it's been written on the blockchain.

The level of distribution and encryption involved means that even if someone were to attempt to hack or change data on the blockchain in any way, the potential costs in terms of cumulative resources would be too high for a single entity or even a well-organized group to attempt, hence it becomes futile and even pointless to attempt it in the first place.

Coins

The general term used to represent cryptocurrencies, for example, meme coins.

Cold Wallet

This is a physical device that is not connected to the internet that you use to store cryptocurrency. Also known as hardware or offline wallets, these devices have a lower risk of compromise compared to online wallets. Examples include solid state drives, hard drives, or flash drives. Note, however, that losing the physical storage device without any other kind of backup could mean your digital assets are lost forever.

Cryptocurrency

Also referred to as crypto, is any kind of virtual or digital currency that can be used as money. Thus, cryptocurrencies can be exchanged for other currencies (fiat or cryptocurrencies) and used to pay for goods or services. Cryptocurrencies use cryptographic encryption to verify, record, and secure transactions, taking away the need for third parties like banks in transactions.

Cryptography

A secure method of communication that involves scrambling information into fragments that cannot be deciphered by anyone apart from the sender and recipient. The encrypted information can only be decrypted with the authentic keys.

DAO

DAO stands for decentralized autonomous organization, which infers a collective of people or entities that come together to pursue shared goals and objectives. DAOs operate as communities but don't have a central authority, in line with the guidelines of blockchain decentralization. The governing rules of DAOs are usually written into the project code and are self-executing when the predetermined conditions are met. Using smart contracts, some of the DAO decisions that are automatically executed include voting, proposals, or even auditing and improving the DAO code.

Decentralization

This is a feature of computing where all responsibility and authority are transferred from a central authority such as a system administrator to a collective of users, whose action is governed by the majority rules built into the computing entity. The point of decentralization is to ensure that no single entity has complete control, or can amass enough participatory influence through other means to control the network.

Decentralized Applications (dApps)

These are digital programs and peer-to-peer applications that exist on blockchain networks. By virtue of decentralization, these apps are not controlled by any central entity and are commonly used as disruptive technologies or solutions in the industries where they are implemented.

Decentralized Finance (DeFi)

This is a modern, blockchain-based approach to banking and financial services that implements trustless and decentralized blockchain functionality to circumvent the role of middlemen like banks and brokers in financial activities. Without intermediaries, DeFi solutions provide faster and more affordable financial services through peer-to-peer payments.

Digital Assets

These are assets that are stored digitally. Most of the digital files you've come across can fit into this description. However, what makes digital assets valuable to their owners is that they must be uniquely identifiable and have distinct access and usage rights. Examples include websites, blogs, emails, slide presentations, and documents with privileged access protocols.

Distributed Ledger Technology (DLT)

This is a digital system for recording and storing transactions across a vast network of computer nodes in different locations. This system allows room for simultaneous updates and validation, and all records added to the network are immutable. The blockchain is one of the best examples of distributed ledger technologies, where information is synchronized and distributed across networks all over the world. Before blockchain technology, information would be stored by a central entity. For example, banks generally store all the transactions in one place, which is quite easy to identify and compromise.

Exchange

An exchange is a marketplace built into an app or website that you can use to trade crypto assets. Crypto exchanges operate in the same way as the normal brokerages in the traditional financial markets, for example, the stock exchange. Thus, you can deposit funds in your local currency and use the deposits to buy cryptocurrency. You can also trade one cryptocurrency for another.

Encryption

This is an elaborate process of securing digital information in a manner that makes it accessible only to those with authorized access. For cryptocurrency, the process involves encryption algorithms and unique keys to verify the authenticity and validity of transactions.

Fiat Currency

Fiat refers to the traditional state-issued currencies like the U.S. dollar, whose values are not backed by any commodities like gold. Governments, through the central banking authorities, use fiat currency to exercise control over the economy, mostly by controlling the amount of money that can be printed. This level of control also helps to control the rate of inflation.

Fork

A fork in blockchain terms refers to an instance where the developers or community involved in maintaining a project decide to change the basic set of rules or protocols of that project. Changing protocols usually creates a new iteration of the project, basically moving in a different direction from the original.

There are two kinds of forks. A soft fork happens when changes made to the project protocols are not too significant and do not change the basic rules of the project. In a soft fork, both the new and old rules are still acceptable on the project and can be used to update the project.

A hard fork, on the other hand, introduces drastic changes that are so significant that the resulting rules are incompatible with the original. Hard forks generally result in the creation of a completely new project.

Forks are necessary when developers or the community involved in a project decide to change or improve some fundamentals of the project. Possible reasons for a fork include disagreement on the vision or future plans for the project, or even the aftermath of a hack.

Gas

This is the user fee necessary to perform a transaction or to fulfill a contract on the Ethereum blockchain. Miners are compensated in gas fees for their actions in securing the platform and verifying transactions. Gas fees can also be seen as a major deterrent to anyone who might attempt malicious action on the network.

Hash

This is a function or a result that is used for securing messages, passwords, or cryptocurrency on the blockchain. Hash functions are an integral part of cryptography, and their level of difficulty and complexity varies according to their roles.

Hashing algorithms are used to compress data into unique strings of alphanumeric text, which support the immutability feature in blockchain computing. Cryptographic hashing makes it possible to identify and flag any attempts to alter records on the blockchain, even in instances of vast amounts of data.

Assuming that someone tries to change any record on the blockchain, they'd have to change all the other consecutive transactions before and after their transaction of interest because all transactions on the blockchain are linked sequentially. This makes cheating on the blockchain an impossibly tedious, frustrating, and pointless attempt.

Hot Wallet

This is an online cryptocurrency wallet, usually provided by third parties or online crypto exchanges. Hot wallets are always connected to crypto networks online, making them prime targets for hacking attempts. Unlike cold wallets, you might be able to regain access to your digital assets if you lose your access codes.

Initial Coin Offerings (ICO)

Initial coin offerings (ICO) are the cryptocurrency version of initial public offerings (IPO). As investors use IPOs to raise capital for a venture, so do investors in cryptocurrencies through ICOs. ICOs are an invitation to the public to buy into a new crypto project by exchanging their money for unique tokens.

Know Your Customer (KYC)

This is a mandatory obligation for financial institutions such as crypto exchanges to perform due diligence and identity checks on their customers. Cryptocurrencies have, for a long time, been plagued with concerns about criminals and other fraudulent entities taking advantage of their anonymity to fund or conduct illegal activities. KYC also plays an important role in verifying customer transactions to ensure they comply with globally accepted counter-terrorism and anti-money laundering (AML) laws.

Mining

This is a highly competitive process for verifying and adding new transactions to the blockchain, particularly for cryptocurrencies like Bitcoin that use the Proof of Work (PoW) consensus algorithm. In this method, the entity that wins the race to mine the next block on the blockchain is awarded some of the newly mined currency and its transaction fees.

The prospect of earning some cryptocurrency excites miners, who are mostly volunteers. The mining process involves trying to guess the closest possible value of a 64-character hash function against trillions of possible combinations within a 10-minute window. This process requires massive computing power, making it impractical for the average home PC user. With the current volatility in Bitcoin prices, mining has become even less attractive to individual miners with expensive computing equipment and is now only feasible for companies with equipment and resources dedicated to mining.

Node

Also known as a blockchain node, a node is a device—for example, a computer—that is connected to other devices on a blockchain network. Every node on the blockchain maintains a copy of the blockchain and supports the network by relaying and validating transactions as they are conducted.

Non-fungible tokens (NFT)

These are unique cryptographic assets on the blockchain that are used to represent items in the real world, like real estate, music, or even art.

Peer-to-Peer (P2P)

This is the direct interaction of two or more entities. In the case of blockchain technology, this is the exchange of digital assets between users without the need for an intermediary. For example, banks act as intermediaries between lenders and borrowers. In the blockchain ecosystem, lenders and borrowers carry out their transactions without banks.

Private Key

In blockchain technology, a private key is the equivalent of a password. Private keys are impossibly long alphanumeric codes used to create digital signatures for verification. They help in authorizing transactions by confirming the authenticity of ownership of an address on the blockchain.

Public Key

A public key is like your physical address. This is the address that people use to send you cryptocurrency. Think of the public key as a bank account number, or your email address. Public keys are usually paired with private keys for authentication and verification. Thus, someone can send you cryptocurrency using your public key, but you can only unlock and receive them using your private key.

Proof of Work (PoW)

This is one of the consensus algorithms used in blockchain technology for verification of transactions on the blockchain. PoW basically attempts to prove that you have the computational capacity to figure out the next hash required to add a new block onto the blockchain. Because PoW is a resource-intensive mechanism, the massive computational power is usually a deterrent to hackers and other malicious actors.

Proof of Stake (PoS)

Unlike PoW, where you must prove you have the computational capacity on the blockchain, PoS requires you to stake coins on the blockchain. You can think of this like a buy-in, where only those who have staked the required number of coins can be validators on the blockchain. While the massive computational capacity is a deterrent in PoW, the disincentive in PoS is that you might lose the coins you staked if you try to deliberately approve an illegal activity on the blockchain.

PoS is also considered relatively safer for the environment compared to PoW because it has comparatively lower energy consumption. On the other hand, the fact that you can stake coins means that users who stake more coins have a higher chance of validating transactions on the blockchain.

Smart Contracts

These are autonomous contracts that self-execute when the terms of the contract are met. The terms are coded into the contract, which then exists on the decentralized blockchain network. Smart contracts eliminate the need for intermediaries or any other kind of intervention to implement a contract. In line with the basic blockchain functionalities, a smart contract cannot be undone or changed once it's been executed.

Stablecoins

These are cryptocurrencies that derive their values from other assets like financial instruments, commodities, fiat currency, or even other cryptocurrencies. Stablecoins are generally used as a buffer against the volatility in the market, especially when trading in cryptocurrencies like Bitcoin, whose prices fluctuate all the time. They are also useful for facilitating transactions in crypto exchanges, whereby instead of buying cryptocurrency with normal currency like the U.S. dollar, you can buy a stablecoin and use it to buy the cryptocurrency you want.

Whitepaper

This is a technical document describing a blockchain project that is usually released by the developers of the project. The whitepaper provides detailed information about the purpose of the project, the technologies behind it, and any other information that might be useful to potential investors to help them understand and buy into the project.

References

American Numismatic Association. (2022). *Chinese Coinage*. Money.org. https://www.money.org/money-museum/virtual-exhibits/hom/case5

Arora, S. (2020, May 12). *What is a Smart Contract in Blockchain and How Does it Work?* Simplilearn.com; Simplilearn. https://www.simplilearn.com/tutorials/blockchain-tutorial/what-is-smart-contract

Bylund, A. (2021). *The Future of Cryptocurrency 2022 and Beyond: Is It the Future of Money?* The Motley Fool. https://www.fool.com/investing/stock-market/market-sectors/financials/cryptocurrency-stocks/future-of-cryptocurrency/

Cartwright, M. (2016, July 15). *Ancient Greek Coinage*. World History Encyclopedia. https://www.worldhistory.org/Greek_Coinage/

Coinbase. (2019). *7 Biggest Bitcoin Myths*. @Coinbase; Coinbase. https://www.coinbase.com/learn/crypto-basics/7-biggest-bitcoin-myths

Ethereum.org. (2020). *Decentralized finance (DeFi) | ethereum.org*. Ethereum.org. https://ethereum.org/en/defi/

Farrington, R. (2020, August 7). *The College Investor*. The College Investor. https://thecollegeinvestor.com/21245/top-10-bitcoin-crypto-investing-sites/

Frankenfield, J. (2022, June 14). *What Is a Crypto Airdrop?* Investopedia. https://www.investopedia.com/terms/a/airdrop-cryptocurrency.asp

Geroni, D. (2021, January 27). *Top 5 Benefits of Blockchain Technology*. 101 Blockchains; 101 Blockchains. https://101blockchains.com/benefits-of-blockchain-technology/

Geroni, D. (2021, November 8). *Different Types of Crypto Wallets – Explained*. 101 Blockchains; 101 Blockchains. https://101blockchains.com/types-of-crypto-wallets/

GWI. (2018). *The future of cryptocurrency: what's next for this craze? - GWI*. Gwi.com. https://www.gwi.com/connecting-the-dots/future-of-cryptocurrency

Haar, R. (2022, May 3). *The Future of Cryptocurrency: 5 Experts' Predictions After a "Breakthrough" 2021*. NextAdvisor with TIME. https://time.com/nextadvisor/investing/cryptocurrency/future-of-cryptocurrency/

Hertig, A. (2020, September 18). *What Is DeFi?* @Coindesk; CoinDesk. https://www.coindesk.com/learn/what-is-defi/

IBM. (2022). *Benefits of blockchain - IBM Blockchain | IBM*. IBM.com. https://www.ibm.com/topics/benefits-of-blockchain

Jones, E. (2022, July 14). *A Brief History of Cryptocurrency - CryptoVantage.* CryptoVantage. https://www.cryptovantage.com/guides/a-brief-history-of-cryptocurrency/

Kusimba, C. (2017, June 20). *When – and why – did people first start using money?* The Conversation. https://theconversation.com/when-and-why-did-people-first-start-using-money-78887

Lanchester, J. (2019, July 24). *The Invention of Money.* The New Yorker; The New Yorker. https://www.newyorker.com/magazine/2019/08/05/the-invention-of-money

Lesso, R. (2022, February 4). *Ancient Roman Coins: How Were They Made?* TheCollector; TheCollector. https://www.thecollector.com/ancient-roman-coins-how-were-they-made/

Lielacher, A. (2022, June 29). *Best Crypto Exchanges.* Investopedia. https://www.investopedia.com/best-crypto-exchanges-5071855

Martucci, B. (2022, April 1). *What Is Cryptocurrency - How It Works, History & Bitcoin Alternatives.* Moneycrashers.com. https://www.moneycrashers.com/cryptocurrency-history-bitcoin-alternatives/

Money Museum. (2022). *The History of Coins in China | moneymuseum.com.* Moneymuseum.com. https://www.moneymuseum.com/en/archive/the-history-of-coins-in-china-123

Pang, K. (2021, August 24). *Chinese Ancient Currency, History of Ancient Chinese Money.* Chinahighlights.com; China Highlights. https://www.chinahighlights.com/travelguide/culture/chinese-ancient-currency.htm

Pratt, M. K. (2021, June 2). *Top 10 benefits of blockchain technology for business.* Tech Target; TechTarget. https://www.techtarget.com/searchcio/feature/Top-10-benefits-of-blockchain-technology-for-business

Reiff, N. (2022, May 21). *Top Cryptocurrency Myths.* Investopedia. https://www.investopedia.com/tech/top-bitcoin-myths/

Sergeenkov, A. (2022, January 18). *What Is a Crypto Airdrop?* @Coindesk; CoinDesk. https://www.coindesk.com/learn/what-is-a-crypto-airdrop/

Sharma, R. (2022, June 26). *Decentralized Finance (DeFi).* Investopedia. https://www.investopedia.com/decentralized-finance-defi-5113835

Sharma, T. K. (2020, July 2). *Types of Crypto Wallets Explained | Blockchain Council.* Blockchain-Council.org. https://www.blockchain-council.org/blockchain/types-of-crypto-wallets-explained/

Srinawakoon, S. (2019, May 14). *Band Protocol — A Protocol for Decentralized Data Governance.* Medium; Band Protocol. https://medium.com/bandprotocol/band-protocol-a-protocol-for-decentralized-data-governance-1ab7f5e2a7c2

Stanford Center for Professional Development. (2020, March 31). *What Does the Future Hold for Cryptocurrency?* Stanford Online; Stanford University. https://online.stanford.edu/future-for-cryptocurrency

Szczepanski, K. (2019, October 17). *The Invention of Paper Money in China.* ThoughtCo. https://www.thoughtco.com/the-invention-of-paper-money-195167

The BitPay Team. (2022, June 14). *Different Types of Crypto Wallets Explained [2022] | BitPay.* The BitPay Blog; The BitPay Blog. https://bitpay.com/blog/types-of-crypto-wallets/#:~:text=The%20two%20most%20popular%20types,way%20of%20securing%20your%20crypto.

Vos, C. (2022, July 14). *What is a crypto airdrop and how does it work?* Cointelegraph; Cointelegraph. https://cointelegraph.com/news/what-is-a-crypto-airdrop-and-how-does-it-work

Wilson, D. (2022). *Ancient Greek Money & Coins Lesson for Kids | Study.com.* Study.com. https://study.com/academy/lesson/ancient-greek-money-coins-lesson-for-kids.html